THE UNSTOPPABLE WOMAN'S MANIFESTO

From Vision to Victory to Building Your Empire

Rochel Marie Lawson

To my radiant, resilient daughter, Lauryn Alexis Marie Lawson - a beacon of boundless potential and endless dreams. Your unwavering spirit, daring curiosity, and passionate heart inspire me daily, filling my soul with hope and tenacity. This is for you, for the lessons I hope you'll learn, for the wisdom I hope you'll gain, and for the legacy I hope you'll continue.

And, to all the fierce, unstoppable women scattered across the globe who dare to envision, construct, master, and broaden their realms of influence. To you who aspire to lead, innovate, challenge, and leave a mark on the world through your entrepreneurship. To you who weather the storm of adversity, rise in the face of hardship, and persist in an ever-changing landscape. To those who balance the scales of personal and professional life, never let the flame of your dreams diminish.

This book is dedicated to you to honor your courage, your grit, and your audacious spirit. I hope these pages guide you, lighting your path as you forge your destiny and empowering you to become the masters of your narratives.

May you never stop dreaming. May you never stop growing. May you never stop breaking barriers. In essence, may you never stop being unstoppable.

contents

INTRODUCTION

My journey to becoming a successful entrepreneur was not a straight path; it was filled with twists and turns, ups and downs, and countless lessons. I have been likened to many historical women who defied their times and pushed boundaries, but none resonates with me more profoundly than Queen Nefertiti.

My name is Rochel Lawson, and like Queen Nefertiti, I have always believed in the power of women. This belief was ingrained in me from my earliest memories, and as I grew, it became a central tenet in my life. Despite being born thousands of years apart, Nefertiti and I share a common ethos:

- An unwavering belief in our abilities to shape our destinies.

- A commitment to excellence.

- The will to empower those around us.

It's no coincidence that Nefertiti's name means a beautiful woman has come,' for her legacy is more than just physical beauty—it's about strength, resilience, leadership, and change. These attributes have defined my journey.

I remember my first venture vividly—a small, handmade jewelry business I started in college. I would spend hours crafting unique pieces, each telling a story of perseverance, hope, and triumph. The endeavor wasn't wildly profitable, but it was my first taste of entrepreneurship, and the exhilaration I felt was unparalleled. Little did I know, this small business was the seed for a vast entrepreneurial empire I would one day build. It was the inception of my personal Nefertiti saga.

Queen Nefertiti was a pivotal figure in Egypt's history. She was not just a queen but a reformer, a visionary, and a leader. She defied traditional norms and sparked a religious revolution, pushing monotheism at a time when polytheism was the norm. Her actions challenged societal expectations, sparking significant change and leaving a legacy that has endured thousands of years. Her beauty was widely celebrated, but her audacity, courage, and resilience made her an enduring figure of inspiration.

Just as Nefertiti embarked on her revolutionary journey, I, too, had my upheavals and transformations. After my initial foray into entrepreneurship, I faced numerous challenges in my career, including financial setbacks, societal prejudices, and self-doubt. However, like Nefertiti, I always kept sight of my purpose. I channeled my resilience and ambition to rise above these hurdles, continuously learning and adapting to realize my dreams. I knew I had a mission, a legacy to build that would inspire and empower women just like me.

I have built my empire with the same audacity and resilience that Nefertiti displayed. I expanded into various industries, from a small jewelry business to creating innovative solutions, embracing change, and making a lasting impact. I have done this while maintaining a fulfilling personal life, juggling roles, and navigating the complex tapestry of female entrepreneurship in the 21st century.

This journey led me to write "The Unstoppable Woman's Manifesto." This book is a testament to every woman who dreams of building her empire. It's a compilation of my lessons learned, strategies, and principles that have helped me grow personally and professionally. Through these pages, you will find the inspiration and tools to achieve your dreams, create a sustainable business, and redefine success on your terms.

In the following chapters, you'll learn how to create a business that operates smoothly without your daily intervention, affording you the financial freedom you deserve. You'll also hear from other unstoppable women who have surmounted the challenges they faced, just like Queen Nefertiti and me.

Remember, being unstoppable is not about avoiding failure or hardship. Instead, it's about rising every time we fall, learning from our mistakes, and using them as stepping stones towards our goals. It's about embracing our inner Nefertiti—acknowledging our strength, resilience, and potential to enact change.

The Unstoppable Woman's Manifesto will guide you through the process of cultivating resilience and ambition. It will help you navigate the unpredictable waters of entrepreneurship, equipping you with practical strategies for overcoming challenges and turning your dreams into reality. You'll be introduced to the core principles underpinning sustainable business practices that promote growth and encourage financial independence.

This book is for you, the woman who is determined to achieve her dreams and leave her mark, the woman who strives to balance a rewarding career with a fulfilling personal life, and the woman who believes in her potential to shape her destiny just like Queen Nefertiti did all those centuries ago. This manifesto is for every woman ready to embark on her journey to becoming an unstoppable force.

Drawing on my experiences and those of other unstoppable women, this manifesto will provide real-world insights into building a flourishing empire. We will delve deep into crucial topics, such as cultivating an entrepreneurial mindset, harnessing innovation, empowering your team, maintaining work-life balance, and more.

The journey to entrepreneurship is challenging and often filled with uncertainties and setbacks. But remember, the same was true for Queen Nefertiti. She faced opposition and criticism but persevered, standing tall in her convictions and leading her people towards a new era.

Similarly, my journey was full of struggles. There were moments of self-doubt when I felt like giving up. But just like Nefertiti, I chose to persevere. I decided to believe in my potential, to push through the barriers and turn my dreams into reality.

Today, as I stand at the helm of my entrepreneurial empire, I look back at my journey with pride. The struggles, setbacks, victories, and triumphs have shaped me into the woman I am today. A woman who, much like Queen Nefertiti, embodies resilience, ambition, and the unyielding determination to succeed.

Now, it's your turn. The following chapters are your roadmap to success. Each one builds on the previous, just as each step on your journey will make towards your ultimate goal. Together, we will explore the principles and strategies to empower you to become an unstoppable woman.

I hope "The Unstoppable Woman's Manifesto" will inspire, motivate, and equip you with the tools you need to realize your dreams. Here's to your journey towards becoming an unstoppable woman and the empire you are about to build. May it be as enduring and impactful as that of Queen Nefertiti.

As we delve into the manifesto, remember this: You are stronger than you think. You are more capable than you believe. And just like Nefertiti, you have the power to change your world. Welcome to your unstoppable journey.

Chapter One
The Vision of a Queen

Embracing Your Inner Queen

ONCE UPON A TIME, a queen named Nefertiti lived in the ancient land of Egypt. She was known for her beauty, grace, and wisdom, but what truly set her apart was her ambitious spirit and unyielding determination to build a thriving empire. I first learned about Queen Nefertiti while studying the annals of history, and her story resonated deeply with me. She faced innumerable challenges, yet she remained steadfast in her pursuit of greatness, just like the modern woman entrepreneur of today.

I remember the first time I encountered a seemingly insurmountable obstacle in my business. I attempted to expand my operations but faced countless setbacks and hurdles that threatened to derail my plans. I thought of Queen

Nefertiti and the trials she had met. How had she overcome these obstacles? What was her secret? As I delved deeper into her story, I realized that her unwavering vision and courageous spirit had propelled her forward.

Recently, we have witnessed world events that have tested the resilience and strength of women entrepreneurs. The global pandemic and its economic fallout have challenged the very foundations of our businesses. Yet, in the face of adversity, many have risen to the challenge, pivoting their operations and adapting to the new normal. Like Queen Nefertiti, these women have harnessed the power of their visions to guide them through the storm.

In this chapter, we will explore the principles that guided Queen Nefertiti in her quest to scale her empire, principles that can be applied by the modern woman entrepreneur to achieve her own goals. We will delve into four key aspects of Queen Nefertiti's vision:

1. **The Visionary Queen:** Developing a clear and concise vision for your empire.

2. **The Courageous Queen:** Overcoming fears and doubts to pursue your dreams.

3. **The Confident Queen:** Building self-confidence to lead your empire.

4. **The Focused Queen:** Staying focused on your goals to

achieve success.

The Visionary Queen: Developing a Clear and Concise Vision for Your Empire

Queen Nefertiti understood the importance of having a powerful vision. Her ability to clearly envision her empire's future allowed her to make strategic decisions and navigate the complexities of her reign. As a modern woman entrepreneur, having a clear and concise vision for your business is paramount. It will serve as a guiding light, helping you make informed decisions and chart the course of your enterprise.

To develop your own visionary prowess, consider the following steps:

a. **Define your purpose:** Ask yourself, "Why does my business exist?" Your purpose is the fundamental reason your company exists beyond simply making a profit. It should inspire you and guide your decision-making process. For example, Queen Nefertiti's purpose might have been to create a thriving, prosperous, and enlightened society.

b. **Identify your core values:** Your core values are the principles that guide your actions and decision-making. They help create your organization's culture and ensure that your business stays true to its purpose. Consider what values are most important to you and how they can be reflected in your company. Queen Nefertiti might have valued innovation, collaboration, and integrity.

c. **Set long-term goals:** Once you clearly understand your purpose and core values, establish long-term goals for your business. These goals should align with your sense and values and be ambitious yet achievable. For instance, Queen Nefertiti's long-term goals included expanding her empire's territory, fostering trade relations, and advancing the arts and sciences.

d. **Create a vivid mental picture:** To truly harness the power of your vision, create a graphic mental image of what success looks like for your business. This mental picture should be so clear that you can almost touch, taste, and smell it. Envisioning your empire's future success will inspire you and motivate your team to work towards realizing that vision.

Remember to be flexible and open to change as you develop your vision. Just as Queen Nefertiti had to adapt to the shifting sands of her time, so must you be willing to revise your vision as your business and the world around you evolve.

The Courageous Queen: Overcoming Fears and Doubts to Pursue Your Dreams

As Queen Nefertiti embarked on her ambitious journey to build a thriving empire, she inevitably faced her fair share of fears and doubts. However, her courage and determination allowed her to conquer these obstacles and forge ahead on her path to success. As an entrepreneur, you, too, will encounter fears and doubts, but it's essential to face them head-on to reach your goals.

Here are some strategies to help you overcome your fears and doubts:

a. **Acknowledge and accept your fears:** The first step to conquering them is acknowledging and accepting them. Understand that feeling fear is normal, especially when starting or growing a business. You can address and take steps to overcome your fears by recognizing them.

b. **Reframe your fears:** Instead of viewing them as insurmountable barriers, try reframing them as opportunities for growth and learning. This shift in perspective can help you approach your fears with a more positive mindset, making it easier to face and conquer them.

c. **Develop a support network:** Surround yourself with people who believe in you and your vision. A strong support network can provide encouragement, guidance, and advice when facing challenges. These individuals can help bolster your confidence and motivate you to push through your fears and doubts.

d. **Take action:** One of the most effective ways to overcome your fears is by taking action. When you progress, even in small steps, you build momentum and gain confidence. As you continue to take action, you'll find that your fears and doubts diminish, and your belief in yourself and your business grows stronger.

e. **Embrace failure:** Understand that failure is a natural part of the entrepreneurial journey. Instead of fearing failure, view it as a learning opportunity. Each time you encounter a setback, analyze what went wrong and use that knowledge to improve and grow. This mindset will help you develop resilience and better equip you to face future challenges.

By embracing your fears and doubts and using them as opportunities for growth, you can follow in Queen Nefertiti's footsteps and build a flourishing empire.

The Confident Queen: Building Self-Confidence to Lead Your Empire

Queen Nefertiti's confidence was a critical factor in her ability to lead her empire effectively. As an entrepreneur, building self-confidence is crucial for your success. A confident leader can make decisions, communicate effectively, and inspire others. Here are some strategies to help you develop the self-confidence needed to lead your empire:

a. **Focus on your strengths:** To build self-confidence, it's essential to recognize and appreciate your strengths. Reflect on your past achievements and the skills that enabled you to succeed. By focusing on your strengths, you'll be better equipped to face challenges and overcome obstacles.

b. **Set realistic goals:** Setting achievable goals is vital for building self-confidence. By setting realistic goals and breaking them down into smaller, manageable tasks, you can progress and experience success. Each accomplishment will help build confidence and propel you toward your larger vision.

c. **Practice positive self-talk:** How you speak to yourself can significantly impact your self-confidence. Be mindful of negative thoughts and beliefs and replace them with positive affirmations. By practicing positive self-talk, you'll cultivate a more confident mindset and be better prepared to handle the challenges of entrepreneurship.

d. **Seek feedback and learn from it:** To build confidence, it's essential to be open to feedback and learn from it. Seek constructive criticism from trusted mentors or peers, and use their insights to grow and improve. By demonstrating a willingness to learn, you'll become more confident in your abilities and more resilient in the face of challenges.

e. **Visualize success:** Visualization is a powerful tool for building self-confidence. By imagining yourself achieving your goals and overcoming challenges, you can create a mental blueprint for success. This visualization can help boost your self-confidence and motivate you to take the necessary steps to make your vision a reality.

By following these strategies, you'll be able to build the self-confidence needed to lead your empire and achieve success, just as Queen Nefertiti did.

The Focused Queen: Staying focused on your goals to achieve success

Queen Nefertiti's unwavering focus was instrumental in her ability to scale her empire. As an entrepreneur, maintaining focus on your goals is critical for success. Here are some tips to help you stay focused and achieve your entrepreneurial dreams:

a. **Set clear goals and priorities:** To maintain focus, it's crucial to have clearly defined goals and priorities. Write down your short-term and long-term objectives, and create a plan to achieve them. Be specific about what you want to accomplish and the timeframe you hope to achieve it. This will help you stay on track and make it easier to measure progress.

b. **Break tasks into smaller steps:** Breaking tasks down into smaller, more manageable steps can help you maintain focus and prevent overwhelm. When facing an enormous task or project, divide it into smaller sub-tasks with specific deadlines. This will give you a clear roadmap for completing the project and help you stay focused on one task at a time.

c. **Minimize distractions:** In today's fast-paced world, distractions are everywhere. To stay focused, identify the distractions that hinder your productivity and take steps to eliminate or minimize them. This may include setting boundaries, such as turning off notifications on your devices, setting specific hours for work and leisure, creating a designated workspace free from distractions, or using productivity tools like time-blocking techniques to help you stay on task.

d. **Schedule regular breaks:** Regular breaks throughout your workday can help you maintain focus and avoid burnout. Use the Pomodoro Technique, which involves working for a set period (typically 25 minutes), followed by a short break (usually 5 minutes). After completing four work sessions, take a longer break (15-30 minutes). This method can help you maintain concentration while allowing you to recharge and relax so you can return to your tasks with renewed energy and focus.

e. **Stay accountable:** Accountability can be a powerful motivator for staying focused on your goals. Share your objectives with a mentor, coach, or peer who can provide support and encouragement. Regular check-ins with your accountability partner can help you stay on track and maintain focus. Additionally, consider joining mastermind groups or entrepreneur communities where you can share your progress and learn from others facing similar challenges.

f. **Practice mindfulness and meditation:** Practicing mindfulness and meditation can help you stay focused by training your mind to concentrate on the present moment. Set aside time each day for mindfulness practice, even just a few minutes. This will help you develop better focus and improve your ability to manage stress and distractions.

By implementing these strategies, you'll be able to stay focused on your goals and make consistent progress toward achieving success, just as Queen Nefertiti did.

Conclusion

In this chapter, we explored the visionary qualities of Queen Nefertiti and how her leadership skills can inspire entrepreneurs in their journey toward success. Embodying a queen's creative, courageous, confident, and focused aspects will help you develop a clear vision for your business, overcome fears and doubts, build self-confidence, and stay focused on your goals.

By embracing the lessons from Queen Nefertiti's reign and implementing the strategies outlined in this chapter, you can embark on your entrepreneurial journey with confidence, resilience, and determination.

Action Steps:

1. **Define your vision:** Take some time to reflect on your aspirations and the impact you want to make with your business. Write down your vision statement and use it to guide your decision-making process.

2. **Overcome fears and doubts:** List your fears and doubts related to your business. Write down a strategy or action step for each fear to help you confront and overcome it. This will empower you to face challenges head-on and move forward with confidence.

3. **Develop self-confidence:** Set achievable goals for yourself and celebrate your accomplishments, no matter how small. Surround yourself with supportive people who believe in you and your vision. Constantly remind yourself of your strengths and capabilities to boost your confidence.

4. **Stay focused on your goals:** Prioritize your tasks and break them down into smaller steps to help you stay focused. Identify and minimize distractions, schedule regular breaks, and practice mindfulness to improve concentration.

5. **Seek accountability:** Share your goals with a mentor, coach, or peer who can provide support and encouragement. Join entrepreneurial communities or mastermind groups to stay accountable, learn from others, and maintain focus on your goals.

By following these action steps, you'll be well on your way to becoming a successful entrepreneur, embodying the spirit and determination of Queen Nefertiti.

Chapter Two

THE MINDSET OF A QUEEN

Cultivating the Royal Mindset

I REMEMBER THAT FATEFUL day with absolute clarity. A day that felt like a hurricane, leaving nothing but destruction in its wake. It was the day I lost the most significant contract of my career, a crucial pillar that held up my entire business empire. As the dust settled around me, I was left with uncertainty and self-doubt, questioning my ability to bounce back from such a devastating loss. But as I stood there amidst the chaos, something stirred within me. A newfound strength and determination that would not only see me through this dark time but would ultimately shape the course of my life and pave the way to unimaginable success.

This story isn't just about me. It's about the countless women who have faced seemingly insurmountable obstacles, only to rise from the ashes, stronger and more resilient than ever. It's about acknowledging the inherent power within each of us and learning to harness that power to propel us towards our goals. In today's world, fraught with uncertainty, adversity, and constant challenges, we need a queen's mindset to survive, thrive, and conquer the odds.

This chapter will share the secrets of developing a queen's mindset. This mindset consists of four vital aspects: The Resilient Queen, The Resourceful Queen, The Strategic Queen, and The Positive Queen. By embracing and embodying these characteristics, you will gain the ability to overcome setbacks and challenges, find creative solutions to problems, develop a long-term strategy for your empire, and maintain a positive mindset in the face of adversity.

So, are you ready to embark on this transformative journey that will forever change how you approach life and business? Are you prepared to delve deep within yourself and unlock the power in your core? If so, let's begin!

Before we delve into the four aspects of a queen's mindset, let's take a moment to understand the importance of mindset in our lives. Our mindset is a powerful tool that shapes our thoughts, beliefs, and actions. It is the lens through which we view the world and the driving force behind our decisions. A positive and empowering mindset can propel us toward greatness, while a negative and limiting mindset can keep us trapped in a cycle of mediocrity.

Now, imagine the mindset of a queen. A queen is the epitome of strength, resilience, and grace. She stands tall in the face of adversity, unyielding and unwavering. Her mind is her most powerful weapon, and she wields it with precision and control. This is the mindset that we, as unstoppable women, must strive to achieve.

The first aspect of a queen's mindset is resilience. The Resilient Queen is no stranger to setbacks and challenges. She has faced her fair share of trials and tribulations but refuses to let them define her. Instead, she learns from her mistakes and uses them as stepping stones towards her ultimate goal. To cultivate resilience, we must learn to view challenges as opportunities for growth and self-improvement rather than insurmountable obstacles. We must also develop the ability to bounce back from failure, armed with newfound knowledge and experience.

The second aspect of a queen's mindset is resourcefulness. The Resourceful Queen is a master of finding creative solutions to problems. She does not throw in the towel or admit defeat when faced with a seemingly impossible task. Instead, she thinks outside the box, utilizing her ingenuity and intelligence to find a way forward. We must learn to tap into our inner creativity and embrace unconventional ideas to become more resourceful. We must also be willing to take risks and push the boundaries of what we believe is possible.

The third aspect of a queen's mindset is strategy. The Strategic Queen is a master planner, always looking several steps ahead and considering the long-term consequences of her actions. She knows that building a successful empire requires careful thought and meticulous planning, and she is not afraid to take her time to ensure that her decisions are well-informed and aligned with her goals. We must learn to think critically and analytically about our business and personal lives to develop a strategic mindset. We must also be willing to adapt and pivot as circumstances change, keeping our eyes firmly fixed on the ultimate prize.

The fourth and final aspect of a queen's mindset is positivity. The Positive Queen is a beacon of hope and optimism, even in the darkest times. She understands that maintaining a positive attitude is crucial to her success, as it allows her to stay focused, motivated, and inspired, even when the going gets tough. To foster a positive mindset, we must learn to cultivate gratitude and appreciate the beauty in our lives. We must also develop the habit of surrounding ourselves with uplifting and supportive individuals who share our vision and encourage us to reach for the stars.

So there you have it, the four aspects of a queen's mindset: resilience, resourcefulness, strategy, and positivity. By embracing and integrating these characteristics into your daily life, you will be well on your way to becoming an unstoppable force, capable of conquering any challenge that comes your way and building a legacy that will inspire and empower generations of women to come.

But remember, developing a queen's mindset is not a one-time event or a quick fix. It is a lifelong commitment to personal growth and self-discovery, a journey that requires dedication, perseverance, and the unwavering belief that you, too, can become the queen you were always meant to be.

As we progress through this chapter, I will provide practical advice, personal anecdotes, and real-world examples to help you cultivate and refine each aspect of a queen's mindset. Together, we will explore the unique challenges and obstacles that women face in today's society and discover how the perspective of a queen can help us overcome these barriers and achieve unparalleled success.

The Resilient Queen

Resilience is the cornerstone of a queen's mindset. It is the ability to bounce back from setbacks, to face challenges head-on, and to emerge stronger than before. It is the unyielding determination to push through adversity, no matter how difficult or overwhelming it may seem.

As women, we face unique challenges and obstacles on our path to success. We often encounter societal expectations and gender stereotypes that can hold us back and prevent us from realizing our full potential. To truly succeed, we must develop the resilience of a queen, able to withstand these challenges and continue moving forward, even when the odds seem stacked against us.

One of the most powerful ways to cultivate resilience is through self-reflection. By reflecting on our experiences, we can identify patterns of thought and behavior that may limit our growth and prevent us from reaching our goals. This process of introspection allows us to learn from our mistakes and failures, using them as opportunities for growth and self-improvement.

A personal story of resilience I hold dear to my heart is that of a client I once worked with. She was a talented and ambitious entrepreneur but faced numerous setbacks in her business, including financial struggles and the loss of key clients. Despite these challenges, she refused to give up, determined to make her dreams a reality.

One day, she came to me, seeking guidance and support. We worked together to develop a plan of action to help her overcome the obstacles and achieve her goals. Through our collaboration, she discovered new ways to approach her business, learned to manage her finances more effectively, and developed a more resilient mindset that allowed her to face adversity with grace and determination.

Today, she is a successful entrepreneur, leading a thriving business that has survived and thrived in adversity. Her journey is a testament to the power of resilience and serves as a powerful reminder of the strength and determination within each of us.

Another inspiring example of resilience can be seen in the countless women who have risen to positions of power and influence in the face of adversity. From trailblazing pioneers like Rosa Parks and Malala Yousafzai to industry leaders like Sheryl Sandberg and Indra Nooyi, these women have faced discrimination, setbacks, and challenges yet have emerged as symbols of strength and resilience.

So, how can you develop the resilience of a queen? Here are some actionable steps to help you on your journey:

1. **Embrace failure as a learning opportunity:** Understand that setbacks and failures are inevitable but also valuable lessons that can help you grow and improve. Learn to view them as opportunities for growth rather than insurmountable obstacles.

2. **Develop a strong support network:** Surround yourself with people who believe in you and your dreams and uplift and support you in adversity. They will help you

stay resilient and focused on your goals.

3. **Cultivate self-awareness:** Regularly engage in self-reflection and introspection to identify areas for growth and improvement. This will enable you to learn from your experiences and build resilience.

4. **Practice self-compassion:** Treat yourself with kindness and understanding, especially in adversity. Recognize that setbacks are a normal part of life and that it is okay to feel vulnerable and imperfect.

5. **Set realistic and achievable goals:** Break down your larger goals into smaller, more manageable steps, and celebrate your progress. This will help you stay focused and motivated, even facing challenges.

By embracing these principles and incorporating them into your daily life, you will be well on your way to developing the resilience of a queen.

In the next section, we will delve into the mindset of the Resourceful Queen. We will explore the importance of creativity and adaptability in problem-solving and how you can harness these qualities to overcome challenges and turn your dreams into reality.

Get ready to unlock the true potential of your inner Resourceful Queen. Discover the innovative strategies and techniques that will empower you to find creative solutions to even the most complex problems, allowing you to thrive in the ever-changing landscape of entrepreneurship and personal growth. Are you prepared to embrace your resourcefulness and rewrite the rules of success?

The Resourceful Queen

The Resourceful Queen is a master of adaptability and creative problem-solving. She knows that in the dynamic world of entrepreneurship, the ability to think outside the box and find innovative solutions to challenges is crucial for success. Embodying the mindset of the Resourceful Queen means being open to new ideas, embracing change, and always seeking fresh perspectives to overcome obstacles and seize opportunities.

One of the most inspiring stories of resourcefulness comes from a client I enjoyed working with. This client was a talented fashion designer passionate about creating unique and sustainable clothing. However, she faced a significant obstacle: the high cost of eco-friendly materials made it challenging to compete with fast fashion brands regarding pricing.

Determined to succeed, she sought my guidance, and together, we embarked on a journey to uncover creative solutions to this challenge. Through extensive research and brainstorming, she discovered an innovative way to source affordable, sustainable materials by partnering with local textile waste recycling facilities. This collaboration allowed her to reduce production costs and create a unique selling point for her brand by promoting its eco-conscious ethos.

Today, her fashion line is thriving, and she has become a trailblazer in the sustainable fashion movement. Her resourcefulness and determination have helped her overcome a significant challenge and contribute to a greater cause, promoting sustainability and ethical consumerism.

Another remarkable example of resourcefulness is the story of Sarah Blakely, the founder of Spanx. With a mere $5,000 in her bank account and no prior experience in the fashion industry, Blakely transformed a simple idea into a billion-dollar empire. Her resourcefulness, tenacity, and willingness to learn from her mistakes allowed her to build a successful business that revolutionized women's shapewear.

So, how can you cultivate the mindset of a Resourceful Queen? Here are some practical steps to help you develop this invaluable skill:

1. **Embrace curiosity:** Foster a sense of curiosity and a thirst for knowledge. Continuously seek new ideas, information, and perspectives to help you grow per-

sonally and professionally.

2. **Develop a growth mindset:** Believe that your abilities and intelligence can be developed through hard work, persistence, and dedication. Embrace challenges as opportunities to learn and grow, not threats to your self-worth.

3. **Practice lateral thinking:** Train your brain to think outside the box by regularly engaging in activities that encouraging creativity and imagination. This might include brainstorming, mind mapping, or engaging in creative hobbies such as painting or writing.

4. **Learn from others:** Seek out mentors, role models, and peers who embody the qualities of the Resourceful Queen. Learn from their experiences and insights, and use their wisdom to guide your journey.

5. **Be adaptable:** Embrace change and be willing to pivot your plans and strategies as circumstances evolve. Recognize that the path to success is rarely linear and that adaptability is a key component of long-term success.

By implementing these strategies and nurturing the mindset of the Resourceful Queen, you will be well-equipped to navigate the ever-changing landscape of entrepreneurship and personal growth. You will develop the skills and confidence necessary to overcome challenges, seize opportunities, and ultimately build a successful and sustainable empire.

In the next section, we will explore the mindset of the Strategic Queen. We will delve into the importance of long-term planning and vision and how you can harness these qualities to create a blueprint for success that will guide you through every stage of your entrepreneurial journey.

Are you ready to embark on a journey towards the realm of the Strategic Queen? In the next section, we'll uncover the secrets of long-term planning and strategic thinking that will empower you to create a roadmap for success, enabling you to navigate the complex world of entrepreneurship with clarity, precision, and unwavering determination. Prepare to unlock your inner strategist and build an empire that stands the test of time.

The Strategic Queen

Embracing the mindset of the Strategic Queen requires a deep understanding of the significance of long-term planning, vision, and strategic thinking. The Strategic Queen knows that constructing an empire demands a lucid roadmap for success, complete with well-defined goals and the essential steps to reach them. By establishing a solid strategic foundation, you can traverse the intricate landscape of entrepreneurship with clarity, precision, and steadfast determination.

I'd like to share a story of a young entrepreneur I had the honor of mentoring, which demonstrates the potency of strategic thinking. She was a budding writer with a vision to develop a digital platform centered around women's empowerment. Although she had the drive and talent, she needed a blueprint to transform her dreams into a tangible reality.

Together, we embarked on a journey to devise a comprehensive strategy for her platform, deconstructing her vision into concrete, achievable milestones. We commenced by defining her target audience and the unique value she would provide for them. Next, we pinpointed the crucial resources, partnerships, and promotional approaches needed to build and expand her platform. By creating a meticulous roadmap, she could systematically implement her plan, overcoming obstacles and adjusting her direction to accomplish her objectives.

Her platform has evolved into a flourishing community, offering support, resources, and motivation to thousands of women worldwide. Her triumph can be credited to her strategic mindset and unwavering dedication to her vision.

To cultivate the mindset of the Strategic Queen and design a roadmap for success, consider implementing the following steps:

1. **Define your vision:** Start by articulating your long-term aspirations and the impact you wish to create through your business. Your vision should be ambitious, inspiring, and indicative of your values and passions.

2. **Break down your goals:** Transform your vision into actionable, quantifiable objectives by breaking it down into smaller, attainable milestones. These milestones should be specific, time-bound, and aligned with your goals.

3. **Identify your resources:** Evaluate the resources and capabilities needed to achieve your objectives, encompassing financial, human, and technological assets. This might involve conducting a thorough analysis of your existing resources and identifying gaps and potential areas for growth.

4. **Develop a strategic plan:** With a clear comprehension of your goals and resources, create a detailed plan outlining the steps and actions necessary to achieve your objectives. This plan should include timelines, responsibilities, and key performance indicators KPIs to monitor your progress.

5. **Foster strategic partnerships:** Identify potential partners and collaborators who can support your journey and help you accomplish your goals. This could include industry experts, mentors, or other entrepreneurs who share your values and vision.

6. **Monitor and adjust:** Regularly review and assess your progress, changing your strategy and actions to stay on track. This might involve refining your goals, re-allocating resources, or pivoting your approach to surmount challenges and seize new opportunities.

By adhering to these steps and nurturing the mindset of the Strategic Queen, you will be well-prepared to create a blueprint for success that will guide you through every stage of your entrepreneurial journey. You will develop the skills and confidence required to make informed decisions, manage risk, and construct a thriving, sustainable empire.

In the concluding section, we will delve into the mindset of the Positive Queen. We will investigate the importance of maintaining a positive outlook in the face of adversity and how fostering resilience and optimism can empower you to overcome barriers, rebound from setbacks, and achieve your goals with unwavering determination.

In Section 4, we will uncover the essential qualities of the Positive Queen, revealing how her unwavering optimism and mental strength can become your secret weapon in the face of adversity. Discover the power of a positive mindset and learn practical techniques to harness this transformative energy to conquer challenges and accelerate your path to success. Are you ready to become the Positive Queen?

The Positive Queen

The Positive Queen reigns supreme over her empire with grace, resilience, and an unwavering belief in overcoming challenges. She understands that success is often forged through the fire of adversity and that a positive mindset is a key to unlocking her full potential. As you embark on your entrepreneurial journey, cultivating the mentality of the Positive Queen will empower you to face obstacles head-on, remain steadfast in the face of setbacks, and, ultimately, achieve your goals with unyielding determination.

Consider the story of a client I had the privilege of coaching, who embodied the spirit of the Positive Queen. She was a single mother striving to balance the demands of raising a family and launching a new business. Despite facing numerous hardships, including financial struggles and time constraints, she never allowed adversity to dampen her spirits. Instead, she embraced a positive mindset, using her challenges as fuel to propel her forward.

With unwavering optimism and a strong support network, she persevered through the difficult times, transforming her fledgling business into a thriving enterprise. Today, she is a shining example of the power of positivity, demonstrating that even in the face of overwhelming odds, a positive mindset can lead to incredible achievements.

To harness the power of the Positive Queen and cultivate a resilient, optimistic mindset, consider implementing the following strategies:

1. **Embrace challenges as opportunities for growth:** Adopt the perspective that challenges are not insurmountable obstacles but opportunities for personal and professional development. By viewing adversity as a chance to learn and develop new skills, you can foster resilience and maintain a positive outlook in the face of setbacks.

2. **Surround yourself with positivity:** Surround yourself with individuals who uplift and inspire you, fostering a supportive network of mentors, friends, and colleagues who share your values and aspirations. By immersing yourself in a positive environment, you can reinforce your optimistic mindset and draw strength from those around you.

3. **Practice gratitude:** Cultivate gratitude by regularly acknowledging and appreciating the positive aspects of

your life. This might involve maintaining a gratitude journal, expressing thanks to others, or simply reflecting on your blessings each day. Focusing on the positives can foster greater happiness and well-being, enhancing your resilience in adversity.

4. **Develop coping strategies:** Equip yourself with an arsenal of effective coping strategies to manage stress and maintain a positive mindset during challenging times. This might include practicing mindfulness, engaging in regular exercise, seeking support from others, or utilizing various stress-reduction techniques, such as deep breathing or progressive muscle relaxation.

5. **Visualize success:** Engage in regular visualization exercises, imagining yourself accomplishing your goals and easily overcoming obstacles. By vividly picturing your success, you can reinforce your belief in your ability to achieve your dreams and enhance your motivation to persevere through challenges.

6. **Maintain perspective:** When confronted with setbacks, remind yourself of the bigger picture and the ultimate goals you are working towards. By maintaining perspective, you can prevent yourself from becoming consumed by negative emotions and remain focused on your long-term objectives.

By embracing these strategies and cultivating the mindset of the Positive Queen, you will develop the mental fortitude and unwavering optimism needed to conquer challenges, overcome setbacks, and achieve your entrepreneurial dreams.

As we conclude this chapter, let us reflect on the powerful mindsets of the Resilient, Resourceful, Strategic, and Positive Queen. Each of these mindsets offers unique strengths and insights, empowering you to navigate the complex terrain of entrepreneurship with grace, determination, and an unbreakable spirit. By embodying these qualities, you can build a formidable empire, leaving a lasting legacy that inspires and empowers others to redefine success on their terms.

In conclusion, the mindset of a queen is indispensable in navigating the complex and often challenging world of entrepreneurship. Embodying the qualities of the Resilient, Resourceful, Strategic, and Positive Queen, you will be equipped with the mental fortitude, resilience, and optimism necessary to rise above adversity, overcome challenges, and create a sustainable, thriving empire. As you embark on your entrepreneurial journey, it is vital to remember that cultivating and maintaining this mindset requires consistent effort and dedication. To fully embody the mindsets of these mighty queens and unlock your potential, consider taking the following detailed action steps:

1. **Conduct a self-assessment:** Reflect on your personal experiences, strengths, and weaknesses. Identify areas where you have displayed resilience, resourcefulness, strategic thinking, positivity and areas that need improvement. Use these insights as a foundation for building a stronger mindset moving forward.

2. **Create a support network:** Surround yourself with like-minded individuals who share your entrepreneurial vision and can provide support, encouragement, and inspiration. Seek out mentors, join networking groups, and attend industry events to build a robust network of connections that will bolster your growth and success.

3. **Set clear, measurable goals:** Establish well-defined personal and professional development goals. Break these goals into manageable steps, create a timeline for achieving them, and regularly assess your progress to stay on track. Remember to celebrate milestones to maintain motivation and a sense of accomplishment.

4. **Develop a growth mindset:** Embrace a continuous learning mindset by actively seeking opportunities for personal and professional growth. Attend workshops, read books, listen to podcasts, and engage in online courses to expand your knowledge and develop new skills relevant to your industry.

5. **Cultivate resilience:** Develop your ability to bounce back from setbacks by reframing challenges as opportunities for growth. When faced with adversity, focus on the lessons learned and the potential for personal and professional development rather than dwelling on negative emotions.

6. **Foster resourcefulness:** Enhance your capacity for creative problem-solving by exposing yourself to new experiences, ideas, and perspectives. Engage in brainstorming sessions, collaborate with others, and challenge yourself to think outside the box when facing obstacles.

7. **Refine your strategic thinking:** Build your strategic prowess by continually assessing your business environment, analyzing trends and competitors, and aligning your long-term objectives with actionable short-term goals. Develop a comprehensive business plan that outlines your vision, mission, and strategies for growth, and revisit it regularly to ensure you remain on track.

8. **Practice positivity:** Cultivate a positive mindset through regular gratitude exercises, mindfulness, and visualization techniques. Focus on the positive aspects of your life and work, and surround yourself with optimistic individuals who inspire and uplift you.

9. **Maintain perspective:** When confronted with setbacks

or challenges, remind yourself of the bigger picture and the ultimate goals you are working towards. By maintaining perspective, you can prevent yourself from becoming consumed by negative emotions and remain focused on your long-term objectives.

As you take these action steps and embody the mindset of a queen, you will be better equipped to face the challenges of entrepreneurship and create a lasting, positive impact on your clients and community. Consider incorporating a daily mantra into your routine to further solidify your commitment to adopting this powerful mindset. This mantra will serve as a constant reminder of your inherent power, strength, and ability to conquer any challenge that comes your way:

"I am a queen resilient, resourceful, strategic, and positive. I embrace adversity as an opportunity for growth and remain steadfast in pursuing my dreams. Through unwavering determination and a fierce belief in my abilities, I will create an unstoppable empire and leave a lasting legacy that empowers and inspires others."

Repeat this mantra daily, either as a part of your morning routine or whenever you need a boost of confidence and motivation. By internalizing its message, you will reinforce your commitment to embodying the mindset of a queen and remind yourself of the power you possess to overcome any obstacle that comes your way.

In conclusion, your success as an entrepreneur is intrinsically tied to the mindset you cultivate. By embracing the qualities of the Resilient, Resourceful, Strategic, and Positive Queen, you are setting yourself up for a future filled with growth, innovation, and empowerment. As you work towards creating a sustainable, thriving empire, remember that the journey is just as important as the destination. Each challenge, setback, and triumph will contribute to your evolution as a leader, a businesswoman, and a queen.

By implementing these action steps and the daily recitation of your empowering mantra, you will find the strength and inspiration necessary to create a legacy that transcends your wildest dreams. By embodying the mindset of a queen, you will transform your own life and the lives of those around you, inspiring future generations of women to reach for the stars and redefine success on their terms.

In pursuing greatness, you will undoubtedly face obstacles, setbacks, and moments of self-doubt. But always remember, you are a queen and queens are unstoppable. With unwavering determination, fierce belief in your abilities, and the mindset of a queen firmly in place, there is no challenge too great or dream too ambitious.

So go forth, fearless queen, and create the unstoppable empire you were destined to build. And as you do, never forget the power, resilience, and strength within you for this unstoppable mindset will guide you on your journey toward greatness and leave a lasting legacy that empowers and inspires others.

Chapter Three
The Power of a Queen

Unleashing Your Inner Power

I T WAS A STIFLING summer day when I met with Jennifer, an ambitious entrepreneur who had built her business from scratch. Jennifer was a single mother of two, juggling her parenting responsibilities with her dreams of creating a thriving business to sustain her family. She had the grit and determination to achieve her goals, but she was struggling to break free from the daily grind of her business.

Jennifer worked tirelessly for years, sacrificing her personal life to pursue her dreams. She knew there was more to life than being shackled to her work, and she was desperate for a change. One day, she shared with me the story of Queen Nefertiti, a powerful and influential queen who had harnessed her power and influence to make a difference in her empire and beyond. Jennifer was inspired by Queen Nefertiti's story and believed that if she could tap into her inner power, she could create the life she had always envisioned.

Together, we worked on strategies to empower Jennifer, and in time, she transformed her business into a well-oiled machine that could run without her constant presence. She created systems and processes, delegated tasks to her team, and built a network of supportive allies and mentors. Jennifer's journey was reminiscent of Malala Yousafzai's advocacy for girls' education and women's rights, as both women harnessed their power to create lasting change.

In this chapter, we will explore the Power of a Queen, drawing inspiration from the stories of Queen Nefertiti and Malala Yousafzai to help you take control of your life and business. We will delve into the following four key aspects:

1. The Empowered Queen: Taking control of your life and business

2. The Influential Queen: Building a network of supportive allies and mentors

3. The Charismatic Queen: Cultivating charisma to inspire others

4. The Visionary Queen: Leveraging your power to make a difference in the world

Are you ready to embark on this journey? If so, let's begin with Section 1.

The Empowered Queen: Taking Control of Your Life and Business

To become an Empowered Queen, you must first believe in your abilities and take responsibility for your life and business. You are the architect of your destiny, and only you have the power to shape it as you see fit. This begins with clearly understanding your goals, values, and vision for the future. The following steps will guide you on your journey towards empowerment and self-mastery:

1. **Define your goals:** A queen knows where she is going and what she wants to achieve. Take the time to establish clear, measurable, and achievable goals for your business and personal life. Start by identifying your long-term vision what do you want to accomplish in the next five, ten, or twenty years? Break down this vision into smaller, more manageable goals that can be achieved within a shorter time frame, such as one year or six months. These goals should be specific, measurable, attainable, relevant, and time-bound SMART, providing a clear roadmap to guide your actions and decisions. Remember, your goals should align with your values and passions,

ensuring that your path is successful and fulfilling.

2. **Prioritize self-care:** A queen understands the importance of self-care and takes the time to nurture her body, mind, and soul. In the fast-paced world of entrepreneurship, it's easy to fall into the trap of constantly pushing yourself to the brink of exhaustion. Incorporate self-care practices into your daily routine to avoid burnout and maintain well-being. This may include exercise, meditation, journaling, pursuing hobbies, or spending quality time with loved ones. By prioritizing self-care, you are investing in your physical and mental health and fostering a greater sense of balance and resilience, which will ultimately contribute to your success.

3. **Establish boundaries:** A queen knows her worth and sets limits to protect her time, energy, and well-being. It's crucial to establish clear boundaries that preserve your mental and emotional space in both your personal and professional life. This may involve learning to say "no" to demands that don't align with your goals and values or creating a schedule that separates your work and personal life. By establishing and maintaining boundaries, you demonstrate self-respect and ensure your energy focuses on what truly matters to you.

4. **Delegate and automate:** A queen only does some things herself; she has a team to support her. As your busi-

ness grows, it's essential to recognize the importance of delegation and automation in achieving long-term success. Delegating tasks allows you to focus on strategic decisions and higher-level tasks, while automation streamlines processes and improves efficiency.

To begin delegating, identify tasks that others can perform and ensure that your team members have the necessary skills and resources to complete them. Provide clear instructions and communicate your expectations while empowering your team to take ownership of their work. Remember, effective delegation frees up your time and fosters a sense of trust and collaboration within your team.

Conversely, automation involves using technology to streamline repetitive tasks and processes, such as invoicing, customer relationship management, and social media scheduling. By automating these tasks, you can save time, reduce the risk of human error, and focus on more strategic aspects of your business.

Cultivating a growth mindset means that a queen understands that personal and professional growth is a lifelong journey. Embrace a growth mindset by continually seeking opportunities to learn, improve, and expand your horizons. This may involve attending workshops, reading books, or connecting with mentors and peers in your industry. By embracing a growth mindset, you develop.

The Influential Queen: Building a Network of Supportive Allies and Mentors

Once you've taken control of your life and business as an Empowered Queen, the next step is to become an Influential Queen. Influence is the capacity to affect the character, development, or behavior of someone or something. In essence, it's about making an impact and leaving a mark. Building a network of supportive allies and mentors enhances your sphere of influence and provides a wealth of resources, advice, and support. Let's delve into the process of becoming an Influential Queen:

1. **Identifying and building relationships with key allies:** I was trying to navigate the business world alone when I was just starting as an entrepreneur. I soon realized that success was a collaborative endeavor. It took a network of allies who supported my vision, offered advice, and helped me reach my goals. I remember meeting Sara, a seasoned entrepreneur who became a trusted ally. She had faced similar challenges, and her insights were invaluable in guiding me through my entrepreneurial journey. Similarly, Queen Nefertiti of Egypt understood the importance of allies. She forged powerful alliances during

her reign, which significantly enhanced her influence and contributed to the prosperity of her empire. Just like Sara and Nefertiti, identify individuals who align with your vision and values and actively work to nurture these relationships.

2. **Seeking mentors:** Mentors are a priceless resource in any industry. They can provide guidance, impart wisdom from their experiences, and help you avoid common pitfalls. For instance, when scaling my business, I sought out John, a successful entrepreneur who had built multiple companies. His mentorship saved me from numerous mistakes and pushed me to think bigger and aim higher. Queen Nefertiti, too, had her mentor in the form of her husband, Pharaoh Akhenaten. Under his tutelage, she learned the intricacies of ruling an empire, which she used to co-rule Egypt effectively. Seek mentors with the knowledge and perspective to elevate your business.

3. **Creating a supportive community:** Communities can offer a sense of belonging, provide opportunities for collaboration, and serve as a platform for shared learning and growth. During my entrepreneurial journey, I found immense value in joining professional networks and online communities to connect with like-minded individuals. Similarly, Queen Nefertiti was known for her strong connection with the people of Egypt, making her a beloved figure in her

community. Create or join communities that align with your interests and values, and actively participate in discussions, events, and initiatives.

4. **Leveraging your influence:** Once you've built a robust network, it's time to leverage your power. This could be through leading initiatives, mentoring others, or using your platform to advocate for causes you believe in. For example, I used my influence to launch a women's entrepreneurship initiative, providing resources and mentorship to aspiring women entrepreneurs. Queen Nefertiti, known for her influence on religious reforms during her time, used her position to promote monotheism, a significant shift in the spiritual practices of ancient Egypt. Leveraging your influence can create meaningful change and reinforce your status as an Influential Queen.

5. **Cultivating trust:** Trust is the bedrock of any relationship, and it's no different in the world of business. Be honest, transparent, and consistent in your interactions to build trust within your network. I recall when a potential partnership fell through due to a misunderstanding. Instead of harboring resentment, I addressed the issue openly and honestly, fostering mutual respect and trust. Queen Nefertiti, revered for her wisdom and integrity, built trust among her people, allies, and counterparts by upholding these virtues.

Building a network of supportive allies and mentors as an Influential Queen provides a solid foundation for your success and influence. In the next section, we will explore how to cultivate charisma as a Charismatic Queen.

As we journey further into your transformation, we embark on a thrilling venture: becoming a Charismatic Queen. Charisma - it's an elusive, magnetic quality that captivates those around you. It's not about being the loudest in the room, but rather, the most memorable. Just as a single spark can start a wildfire, your charisma can inspire many, driving them towards a shared vision. Let's unravel the mysteries of cultivating appeal to inspire and lead others effectively.

The Charismatic Queen: Cultivating Charisma to Inspire Others

Once you've built your network as an Influential Queen, the next progression is to develop your charisma as a Charismatic Queen. Charisma is an enchanting blend of confidence, eloquence, authenticity, and a dash of mystery. The unique spark sets you apart, captures attention, and leaves a lasting impression. In this section, we'll explore the traits of a Charismatic Queen and how to cultivate them:

1. **Authenticity:** Authenticity is the cornerstone of

charisma. It's about being genuine and authentic to yourself, which in turn earns the respect and admiration of others. For instance, when pitching to a group of investors, I chose to be transparent about my challenges and my plans to overcome them. This authentic approach was well received, allowing me to secure funding for my venture. Queen Nefertiti, recognized for her genuine concern for her subjects, won the hearts of her people with her authenticity.

2. **Confidence:** Confidence is an essential ingredient of charisma. It's about trusting your abilities and radiating this self-assured energy to those around you. As I began to gain more experience as an entrepreneur, my confidence grew. When I walked into a meeting, I felt assured, not because I knew everything but because I trusted in my ability to figure things out. Similarly, Queen Nefertiti displayed her confidence through her monumental decisions, earning her a place in history as one of the most influential queens.

3. **Empathy:** Empathy is the ability to understand and share the feelings of others, a trait that can dramatically enhance your charisma. I learned this during a challenging period in my business when my team was struggling with a complex project. Instead of dismissing their difficulties, I listened to their concerns, offered solutions, and shared my experiences overcoming similar challenges. This empathetic ap-

proach boosted morale and fostered deeper connections with my team. Queen Nefertiti was known for her compassionate rule, often seen in her depictions of interacting with her subjects, showing empathy towards their hardships.

4. **Eloquence:** Eloquence is the art of effective, expressive communication. It's about articulating your thoughts and ideas in a way that resonates with others. Over time, I honed my communication skills and improved my ability to convey my vision, persuade investors, and motivate my team. Queen Nefertiti, as depicted in the ancient texts, was known for her eloquence and persuasive speech, which played a crucial role in implementing the religious reforms during her reign.

5. **Inspiration:** As a Charismatic Queen, your charisma should inspire others. Whether leading a team, speaking at an event, or negotiating a business deal, your appeal can motivate others to strive for greatness. In my journey, sharing my experiences, successes, and failures can inspire others to pursue their dreams. Queen Nefertiti's life is a timeless inspiration, embodying strength, resilience, and grace. Cultivating charisma as a Charismatic Queen can significantly enhance your impact and influence, personally and professionally. In the next section, we'll delve into leveraging your power as a Visionary Queen to make a difference in the world. Just as a well-crafted

melody leaves an echo in your mind, a Charismatic Queen leaves an indelible imprint on the hearts of others. Beyond merely attracting attention, charisma has the power to build trust, inspire action, and form deep connections. So, how does one genuinely embody charm? Let's delve deeper into the qualities that enhance charisma.

6. **Active Listening:** A charismatic individual is a skilled speaker and a focused listener. People tend to gravitate towards those who genuinely listen to them. Active listening involves entirely focusing on the speaker, understanding their message, and responding thoughtfully. During one of my networking events, I conversed with a fellow entrepreneur. By actively listening and responding with interest, I was not only able to learn valuable insights but also formed a positive, lasting connection.

7. **Positivity:** A charismatic person radiates positive energy. Maintaining a positive outlook, especially in adversity, can be incredibly inspiring. Amidst one of the most challenging phases in my career, when a significant deal fell through, I chose to remain positive. My determination and optimism inspired my team and kept our spirits high, eventually leading us to explore new opportunities.

8. **Presence:** Charisma also involves being fully present in the moment. Whether in a meeting, a networking

event, or a casual conversation, giving your complete attention demonstrates respect and interest. Queen Nefertiti, for instance, was known for her attentive nature towards her subjects, further enhancing her charismatic appeal.

9. **Adaptability:** A Charismatic Queen is adaptable and flexible. It's about navigating through various situations with grace and resilience. When my company underwent a significant shift in business strategy, I embraced the change with adaptability. Despite initial hiccups, I was able to lead my team effectively through this transition.

Charisma, much like a diamond, is multi-faceted. It's not merely about charming others but about genuinely connecting with them. It involves a delicate balance of confidence and humility, eloquence and active listening, authenticity and adaptability. By cultivating these traits, you can become a Charismatic Queen, capable of inspiring others and making a lasting impact.

As we progress to the next section, remember charisma is not a static trait but a dynamic, evolving quality. Cultivating appeal is an ongoing journey, one that will enhance not only your leadership skills but also your personal growth.

The Visionary Queen: Leveraging Your Power to Make a Difference in the World

In the ever-changing world of business, adaptability and foresight are key. But what sets a successful entrepreneur apart is vision - the ability to not just imagine a better future but to act upon it, to lead others towards it. This is the realm of the Visionary Queen. Are you ready to embrace this influential role and shape the destiny of your empire? Let's step into the world of the Visionary Queen and unravel the secrets to leveraging your power to make a difference.

1. **Recognize the Power of Vision:** The Visionary Queen understands that her vision is her most potent tool. It shapes her actions, directs her decisions, and fuels her passion. When I started my first business, I had a clear vision: to create an enterprise that empowers women and fosters innovation. Every step I took every decision I made, was driven by this vision.

2. **Cultivate a Future Focus:** Visionary leaders don't just respond to the present; they shape the future. They are innovators and trailblazers, constantly pushing boundaries and challenging the status quo. When I decided to expand my business, I didn't just consider the current market trends; I envisioned the future landscape of my industry. This future focus enabled me to pioneer innovative solutions and stay ahead of

the curve.

3. **Communicate Your Vision:** As a Visionary Queen, your role is not just to conceive a vision but to articulate it effectively. When Queen Nefertiti introduced a new religion to her kingdom, she didn't merely implement it; she communicated her vision, reasoning, and passion to her people. This communication made her dream accessible and relatable, enabling her to usher in a new era in Egyptian history.

4. **Foster Collective Ownership:** The Visionary Queen doesn't just share her vision; she invites others to participate. She encourages her team to take ownership, empowering them to contribute their ideas and perspectives. In my business, I have always fostered a culture of collective ownership. By involving my team in the decision-making process, I could tap into diverse insights and ideas, thereby enriching our collective vision.

5. **Navigate Change with Grace:** The path to realizing a vision is often strewn with obstacles and unexpected changes. But the Visionary Queen navigates these with grace and resilience. When my business faced a significant challenge, I didn't let it deter me. Instead, I viewed it as an opportunity to learn, adapt, and emerge stronger.

The Visionary Queen leverages her power to make a difference in her business and the world. By recognizing the power of vision, cultivating a future focus, communicating your vision, fostering collective ownership, and navigating change with grace, you can step into the role of a Visionary Queen.

We've journeyed together through empowerment, influence, charisma, and vision, revealing the influential roles within you - the Empowered Queen, the Influential Queen, the Charismatic Queen, and the Visionary Queen.

Embracing Your Inner Queen and Forging Ahead

You've embarked on a transformative journey, traversing through the realms of empowerment, influence, charisma, and vision. These facets form the cornerstone of a prosperous, resilient, and visionary entrepreneur. The Empowered Queen within you takes charge, the Influential Queen builds robust networks, the Charismatic Queen inspires, and the Visionary Queen envisions and brings to life a better future. These roles intermingle, creating an entrepreneur ready to conquer the world and leave an enduring legacy.

Let's take a moment to reflect on the key takeaways from this chapter. Understanding the significance of these roles, how they intertwine, and how you can imbibe them in your life is your stepping-stone to becoming a phenomenal entrepreneur. The time has come to turn these insights into actions, and here are your action steps:

- **Action Step 1:** Assess Your Current Standing - Take stock of where you are in your entrepreneurial journey. Are you the captain of your ship, or are you allowing external factors to steer you off course? Identify areas where you must take charge and consciously try to regain control.

- **Action Step 2:** Expand Your Network - Reach out to other entrepreneurs, mentors, and thought leaders in your field. Building a supportive network can provide you with invaluable insights and resources.

- **Action Step 3:** Cultivate Charisma - Work on your communication and interpersonal skills. A magnetic personality can inspire your team and draw allies to your cause. Remember, charisma isn't about being the loudest in the room; it's about making others feel heard and valued.

- **Action Step 4:** Create a Vision Board - Put your vision into a visual form. A vision board can constantly remind you of your goals and aspirations, motivating you to stay on track.

- **Action Step 5:** Be Open to Change - Understand that your journey will be marked by shifts and unexpected turns. Be resilient and adaptable, viewing these changes as opportunities for growth and learning.

Armed with these action steps, you are ready to unleash your inner Queen and embark on your path to success. Remember, the journey to becoming a Queen is a continuous learning, growing, and evolving process. There will be challenges, but the ability to rise every time you fall makes you unstoppable.

As we conclude this chapter, let's affirm our commitment to our journey with this powerful mantra:

"I am an Empowered Queen, an Influential Queen, a Charismatic Queen, and a Visionary Queen. I embrace these roles, harness my strengths, and rise above challenges. I am unstoppable."

Carry this mantra with you as you forge ahead, ready to conquer the world and leave an indelible legacy. Embrace your power, fellow Queen, for you are truly unstoppable.

Chapter Four

THE DISCIPLINE OF A QUEEN

The Art of Royal Discipline

As a seasoned entrepreneur, I have realized the immeasurable value of discipline. The same force propelled historical icons such as Queen Nefertiti to unprecedented heights, the relentless pursuit of her vision to expand her empire, a testament to her unwavering discipline.

Like Nefertiti, my journey in entrepreneurship wasn't handed to me on a silver platter. I fought for every milestone, every contract, and every satisfied client. My ambition was my compass, but my discipline was my fuel.

The understanding of discipline's importance was a hard-earned lesson. At a time when my business was beginning to take off, I found myself overwhelmed. I was putting out fires daily, dealing with countless unforeseen problems. My health and relationships started to suffer.

To salvage what was left, I decided to embrace discipline fully. I instituted systems and processes, developed a laser-focused commitment, optimized my productivity, and built resilience in the face of challenges. The results were transformative. My business became a well-oiled machine, and I found a renewed sense of fulfillment.

This story echoes the journey of Serena Williams, a woman who exhibited intense discipline in her career. Her consistent rise in tennis and relentless drive to stay at the top testify to discipline's power.

The promise to you, as you traverse your entrepreneurial journey, is that adopting this same discipline will transform your empire.

In this chapter, we will delve into the core tenets of discipline. We will explore:

1. The Organized Queen: Creating systems and processes for efficient operations.

2. The Committed Queen: Staying committed to your goals through discipline.

3. The Productive Queen: Maximizing your time and

energy for maximum productivity.

4. The Persevering Queen: Overcoming obstacles and persevering through challenges.

Have you ever imagined what it would feel like to have your business running smoothly like a well-oiled machine, where every cog and piece fits perfectly? Let's explore how creating systems and processes can make that dream a reality.

The Organized Queen: Creating Systems and Processes for Efficient Operations

Organization becomes a beacon of hope in a world where chaos can often reign. Like Queen Nefertiti's, systems and processes are the building blocks of any successful empire. Her kingdom, one of the most prosperous and influential of its time, didn't attain such heights by chance. It was meticulously planned and executed, a result of carefully curated systems and processes that were put in place. This level of organization allowed her to rule effectively, making monumental strides in art, culture, and economy.

Drawing a parallel to my journey, I also faced similar hurdles. When my business was in its infancy, I was the linchpin holding everything together. I was involved in management, finances, marketing, and customer service. A maelstrom of tasks left me stretched thin, my efforts diluted.

The turning point came when I understood the power of systems and processes. I started by identifying the areas in my business that were eating up most of my time. Mundane tasks such as invoicing, tracking payments, scheduling meetings, and customer follow-ups consumed much of my day.

With this clarity, I started implementing systems to streamline these tasks. For instance, I employed financial software for invoicing and payment tracking. I used a project management tool to track project milestones, deadlines, and delegation of tasks to my team. I leveraged an automated scheduling tool for meetings, saving me from the endless back-and-forth emails.

With these systems in place, my day-to-day operations began to run more smoothly. It freed up my time and allowed me to focus on high-impact business areas, like strategizing growth and nurturing client relationships.

This new organizational shift reminded me of Nefertiti's empire, where each system had a role, each process, and a purpose. Her dedication to creating a thriving culture was seen in meticulously planning architectural marvels and promoting the arts. Similarly, having a detailed system for each operation can contribute to creating a flourishing empire.

But creating systems isn't just about business operations. It also extends to personal productivity. For example, I incorporated a unique method for time management modeled after the Pomodoro technique. I would work diligently for 25 minutes and then take a 5-minute break. This ensured I wasn't burning out and kept my productivity levels high. I also set a daily ritual to plan my day every morning, aligning my tasks with my overall goals.

The implementation of these systems and processes took time to happen. It was a gradual process that required trial and error. However, the impact it had on my business was palpable. It allowed me to expand my business without getting overwhelmed. It provided a framework for my team to follow, reducing confusion and increasing productivity.

To conclude this section, systems, and processes are the organizational backbone of any successful venture. They free up your time, improve productivity, and facilitate business growth. Much like Queen Nefertiti, whose well-structured empire left a lasting impact, embedding robust systems and processes into your business will undoubtedly pave the way to your entrepreneurial success.

How much are you willing to endure for your dreams? A question that sets apart the dreamers from the achievers. Commitment isn't just about pledging your loyalty to a cause; it's about standing firm in the face of adversity, marching on even when the odds are stacked against you.

The Committed Queen: Staying Committed to Your Goals Through Discipline

Much like a ship requires an unwavering compass to navigate the tumultuous seas, an entrepreneur requires a steadfast commitment to guide their venture through uncertain terrains. Queen Nefertiti's reign is a testament to this. Known for her strong commitment to the cultural revolution and religious transformation, Nefertiti persisted despite traditionalist resistance. Her unwavering commitment to her vision led to flourishing art, culture, and spirituality during her reign. Her reign became synonymous with prosperity and advancement, underpinning the power of commitment in shaping one's destiny.

Drawing parallels to my own journey as an entrepreneur, commitment was my north star, guiding me through the labyrinth of challenges and hurdles. I recall when my business was hit by a sudden economic downturn. Orders were dwindling, and maintaining the operational costs took more work. I faced two options- shut down or weather the storm.

It was a trying period, but my commitment to my venture and the people it served was unwavering. I chose to weather the storm.

My commitment translated into action. I started by reevaluating my business model and identifying areas where costs could be reduced without compromising on the quality of service. I pivoted towards more digital marketing strategies to reach a wider audience at lower prices. I also invested in nurturing relationships with existing customers, understanding their needs better, and providing personalized solutions. This customer-centric approach not only helped retain existing customers but also garnered referrals, thereby attracting new customers.

The road to recovery was arduous and fraught with challenges. There were moments of self-doubt and despair, but the guiding light of commitment kept me on track. And, much like the prosperous reign of Nefertiti following her dedicated reformations, my business started showing signs of recovery. The customer base was growing, orders were increasing, and slowly but steadily, the company was pulling itself out of the downturn.

Staying committed to your goals requires discipline. It requires setting clear objectives, creating action plans, and persisting in adversity. Discipline is about making choices that align with your goals, even when they are hard. It's about preceding immediate gratification for long-term success.

One way to foster discipline is through daily habits that align with your goals. For instance, if your goal is to grow your business, a daily practice could be dedicating a specific time for business development activities like networking, researching market trends, or strategizing growth plans.

Another critical aspect of commitment is resilience. The path to achieving your goals will only sometimes be smooth. There will be obstacles, failures, and setbacks. Resilience is about returning from these challenges and pursuing your goals with renewed vigor.

In conclusion, staying committed to your goals is a defining characteristic of successful entrepreneurs. It requires discipline, resilience, and a relentless pursuit of your objectives. Like Queen Nefertiti, whose commitment to her vision revolutionized an empire, your unwavering commitment to your goals can propel your business to unprecedented heights.

Can you imagine a queen idling away in her palace, oblivious to her realm? Of course not! The true queen isn't just a figurehead she's a paragon of productivity, expertly balancing multiple responsibilities and tasks. Time, after all, is the essence of entrepreneurship.

The Productive Queen: Maximizing Your Time and Energy For Maximum Productivity

Productivity is the lifeblood of entrepreneurship. It's not about cramming more tasks into your day but strategically using your time and energy to create maximum value. The effectiveness of a queen isn't gauged by the hours she spends on the throne but by the impact of her decisions and actions.

Queen Nefertiti, the beautiful and wise ruler of Egypt, exemplified productivity. Amidst her manifold duties, she revolutionized Egyptian culture and religion. Her decisive actions, even when met with resistance, led to cultural flourishing during her reign. She did not squander her time in indecisiveness or procrastination but executed her duties precisely and efficiently, maximizing her productivity.

Just as Queen Nefertiti maximized her productivity for her kingdom's prosperity, so did I strive to do the same in my entrepreneurial journey. Running a business is like juggling multiple balls. There's marketing, sales, operations, finance, and countless other tasks. It can be overwhelming, especially when striving to balance work and personal life.

Early in my entrepreneurship journey, I learned the importance of prioritizing tasks. Not all tasks are created equal.

Some have a more significant impact on your business growth than others. By identifying these high-impact tasks and focusing my energy on them, I was able to achieve more in less time.

One of the tools that aided me in this process was the Eisenhower Matrix, a simple yet effective tool for task prioritization. It divides tasks into four categories based on their urgency and importance. The aim is to focus on important but not urgent tasks, thereby preventing them from becoming urgent crises in the future.

Another crucial aspect of productivity is delegation. As an entrepreneur, it's natural to want to oversee every aspect of your business. However, this can lead to burnout and decreased productivity. Delegation frees up your time for strategic tasks and empowers your team members by entrusting them with responsibilities.

In my entrepreneurial journey, delegating tasks to my team members was a game-changer. It allowed me to focus on strategic tasks that could drive business growth while ensuring that other tasks were adequately handled. It was difficult to relinquish control, but the results were worth it.

Similarly, leveraging technology can significantly boost productivity. From project management tools to automating repetitive tasks, technology can save valuable time and resources. Implementing a Customer Relationship Management CRM system in my business streamlined our sales process, increased efficiency, and improved customer service.

Lastly, maintaining a healthy work-life balance is essential for sustained productivity. Overworking can lead to burnout and decrease productivity in the long run. Therefore, it's crucial to take care of your physical and mental health, engage in activities you enjoy, and spend time with loved ones.

In conclusion, maximizing your productivity is about working smarter, not harder. It involves prioritizing tasks, delegating responsibilities, leveraging technology, and maintaining a healthy work-life balance. As with Queen Nefertiti, whose practical actions led to a cultural renaissance, your productivity can fuel your business growth and personal fulfillment.

Perseverance is the queen's secret weapon. Not the absence of challenges makes a queen, but her relentless determination to overcome them. In the face of adversity, the queen does not buckle but rises with resilience and courage. But how does she do it? And more importantly, how can you, as an entrepreneur, harness this power of perseverance?

The Persevering Queen: Overcoming Obstacles and Persevering Through Challenges

In the grand tapestry of entrepreneurship, perseverance stands as a vivid thread. It paints a picture of relentless determination, unwavering grit, and unyielding courage, weaving through the countless challenges that arise on the journey to success. As the famous American industrialist Henry Ford once said, "When everything seems to be going against you, remember that the airplane takes off against the wind, not with it."

The annals of history offer us a compelling example of perseverance in the life of Queen Nefertiti. Reigning during one of the most contentious times in Egyptian history, she faced opposition and controversy as she and her husband, Pharaoh Akhenaten, radically transformed Egyptian religion and culture. Despite these challenges, Nefertiti persevered, remaining steadfast in her conviction and ultimately leading her kingdom to a period of unrivaled prosperity and artistic splendor.

Like Queen Nefertiti, my journey of entrepreneurship has been replete with challenges. Early on, I faced significant hurdles, from financial constraints to market acceptance and competition. Sometimes, I questioned my decisions and doubted my ability to steer the business toward success. Yet, I knew deep within me the spirit of an entrepreneur, a queen, was unwilling to admit defeat. I had a vision for my business and was determined to bring it to fruition, regardless of the challenges in my path.

Our company was on the brink of financial collapse during one challenging period. We had invested heavily in a new product, only to have it fail miserably in the market. The financial loss was severe, and it threatened the very existence of our business. However, instead of succumbing to despair, I saw this failure as a stepping stone, a learning experience. I analyzed our mistakes, took corrective measures, and emerged stronger than before.

Perseverance doesn't mean you won't encounter failures or make mistakes; you won't let them define or deter you from your path. The inner resilience to bounce back from setbacks and the unwavering commitment to your vision enable you to turn obstacles into stepping stones.

One of the most empowering ways to build perseverance is to cultivate a growth mindset. This concept, developed by psychologist Carol Dweck, posits that individuals who believe their abilities can be developed through hard work, good strategies, and input from others have a growth mindset. They tend to achieve more than those with a more fixed mindset those who believe their abilities are innate gifts and fixed traits. A growth mindset enables you to view challenges as opportunities for growth rather than threats to your success.

Another crucial aspect of perseverance is self-belief. Trust in your abilities and your vision. Even when others doubt you or your ideas, stand firm. Your conviction can be the driving force that propels you forward amidst adversity. Remember, every successful entrepreneur faced rejection and criticism, from Steve Jobs to Oprah Winfrey. Yet, they believed in themselves and their ideas, and they persevered.

Lastly, perseverance requires patience. Success doesn't happen overnight. It's a gradual process, one step at a time. Sometimes, progress may be slow, but remember, as long as you're moving forward, you're one step closer to your goal.

Essentially, the queen's perseverance is about resilience in adversity, a growth mindset, self-belief, and patience. Your journey may be challenging, but perseverance, like Queen Nefertiti and countless other successful entrepreneurs, can steer you toward your vision.

As we come to the close of this chapter, let us revisit the invaluable lessons gleaned from the discipline of a queen. How can these insights drive you forward on your entrepreneurial journey, empowering you to create a sustainable business empire? How can they instill within you the resilience to tackle challenges and the wisdom to balance personal and professional commitments effectively? Let's delve deeper.

As we traverse the rugged terrain of entrepreneurship, the invaluable lessons we've extracted from the discipline of a queen remain our guiding beacon, illuminating the path to success and fulfillment. We've observed the embodiment of the Organized Queen in the systems and processes we've adopted, orchestrating an efficient and productive business environment.

We've mirrored the Committed Queen in our unwavering dedication to our goals, pressing forward despite the hurdles that obstruct our path. We've exemplified the Productive Queen in our unceasing quest for efficiency, striving to extract maximum yield from every minute we devote to our ventures. Finally, we've lived the experience of the Persevering Queen, standing tall and unyielding in the face of adversities, converting stumbling blocks into stepping stones for growth and advancement.

Reflect upon the legendary Serena Williams, whose indomitable spirit and unswerving commitment to her craft have propelled her to the pinnacle of her sport. Consider the resilience of Queen Nefertiti, whose reign amidst profound upheaval ushered in a golden era in Egyptian history. Now, gaze upon your own journey as an entrepreneur. Embrace the trials, the triumphs, and the teachings as integral facets of your growth and evolution. They are the threads that weave the unique tapestry of your entrepreneurial journey.

Remember, balancing your professional pursuits and personal commitments is paramount. As an entrepreneur, it's easy to get swept away in the roaring tide of responsibilities and overlook the importance of nurturing our personal lives. To embody the discipline of a queen, we must always remember that success isn't solely defined by professional achievement but also by the quality of our relationships and personal growth.

To encapsulate and implement the insights from this chapter, here are five comprehensive action steps:

1. **Organize Your Kingdom:** Invest in streamlining your processes and implement systems that automate routine tasks. Trello, Asana, or Monday can help manage tasks, monitor progress, and uphold deadlines.

2. **Commitment to Your Crown:** Set lucid, measurable goals, and pledge your allegiance to achieve them. Utilize the SMART Specific, Measurable, Achievable, Relevant, Time-bound framework to structure your plans.

3. **Maximize Your Reign:** Employ productivity tools and techniques like the Pomodoro Technique, time-blocking, and Eisenhower Matrix to prioritize tasks based on urgency and importance.

4. **Persevere Through Storms:** Cultivate a growth mindset

and build resilience. Mindfulness practices, emotional intelligence, and self-care activities can assist in managing stress and maintaining a positive outlook.

5. **Balance Your Scepter:** Establish a work-life balance that caters to your needs. Regularly allocate time for relaxation, hobbies, and spending time with loved ones. Remember, a well-rested mind is a productive one.

As we draw the curtain on this chapter, remember that the journey to building a sustainable empire is demanding, but with the discipline of a queen, it's one you are fully capable of undertaking. Draw from your inner reserves of strength, resilience, and determination, and, like the great Queens and successful entrepreneurs before you, navigate your way to enduring success.

It's time to take these lessons to heart and translate them into action. Stand tall, seize your scepter, and rule your empire with the discipline, resilience, and wisdom of a queen. The mantra that encapsulates this chapter, one that I urge you to take with you on your entrepreneurial journey, is:

"With the discipline of a queen, I create, I commit, I maximize, I persevere, and I balance. I am unstoppable."

This mantra is a testament to your tenacity, ambition, and unfailing dedication to succeed. It acknowledges the struggle and strain often intertwined with entrepreneurship, but more importantly, it glorifies the strength, resilience, and discipline with which you meet these challenges.

The discipline of a queen is not about perfection; it's about growth, it's about resilience, and it's about continuously striving to evolve and improve. This discipline becomes the driving force that fuels your entrepreneurial journey, pushing you to transcend boundaries, shatter ceilings, and redefine success.

This chapter is a testament to your incredible journey as an entrepreneur. It captures the essence of your struggles, triumphs, learnings, and growth. Each section, each example, and each action step is a piece of a giant puzzle that, when put together, forms a roadmap to success, suffused with the discipline, resilience, and the unstoppable spirit of a queen.

But your journey doesn't end here. It's a perpetual, evolving saga of transformation, innovation, and growth. And with the discipline of a queen etched into your spirit, there's no summit too high, no challenge too overwhelming, and no goal too ambitious.

As we conclude this chapter, remember every step you've taken, every challenge you've overcome, and every goal you've achieved has brought you one step closer to the apex of your potential. Embrace the journey, embody the discipline, and let the reign of your empire reflect the queen you are.

In essence, the lessons we've gleaned from the discipline of a queen form the cornerstone of successful entrepreneurship. They become the prism through which we perceive and navigate the complex landscape of entrepreneurship, guiding us in our decision-making processes, influencing our strategies, and shaping our approach to overcoming challenges. They become the compass that navigates us toward our goals, always pointing us in the right direction, even amidst the most tempestuous storms.

Recall this mantra whenever you face adversity, doubt clouds your judgment or your resolve wavers. Let it serve as a reminder of your strength, your capability, and your potential. Let it inspire, motivate, and guide you toward success and fulfillment.

"With the discipline of a queen, I create, I commit, I maximize, I persevere, and I balance. I am unstoppable."

And remember, every word you utter, every decision you make, and every action you take brings you one step closer to realizing your dreams. You are the queen of your destiny, and with the discipline of a queen coursing through your veins, there's no stopping you. The world is your oyster, and your empire is yours to create, nurture, and grow.

Chapter Five
THE CREATIVITY OF A QUEEN

The Vibrancy of Royal Creativity

IN THE VAST, GOLDEN sands of ancient Egypt, where history unfolded beneath the watchful gaze of the gods, a woman of immense wisdom and beauty reigned beside her king. Queen Nefertiti, a figurehead of grace and power, was known for her innovative problem-solving approach and ability to inspire those around her. Her name, meaning "the beautiful one has come," echoed her stunning beauty and the influence she wielded over her kingdom. As a queen, she ruled with compassion and empathy, employing creative strategies to overcome the challenges that faced her people.

Nefertiti was a political figure and a patron of the arts, fostering a cultural renaissance during her time on the throne. Her innovative spirit and vision led to the flourishing of art, architecture, and poetry, leaving a lasting impression on the world. Her legacy is a testament to the power of creativity in shaping history and transforming the lives of those it touches.

In this chapter, we will explore the creative essence of a queen and how you, too, can harness your inner Nefertiti to forge a path to success in your own entrepreneurial journey. By tapping into your innate creativity, you can uncover new opportunities, develop unique solutions to challenges, and create a lasting impact in your field.

As we journey through time, leaving behind the sun-drenched sands of Egypt, we find ourselves amid another powerful woman's creative genius. This woman would go on to leave an indelible mark on literature and civil rights. Maya Angelou, the American poet and writer, penned works that captured the human spirit's pain, struggle, and resilience, inspiring generations of women to rise above adversity and embrace their creative potential.

Angelou's words, rich in visceral and emotional language, resonated with countless readers. Her empathetic and motivational tone allowed her to speak to the pain and struggles faced by many, especially women in American society. Her resilience, strength, and ambition were evident in her work, serving as a beacon of hope and inspiration to those who encountered her writing. She embraced creativity as a powerful tool for change, and her legacy continues to empower and inspire women worldwide.

In this chapter, we will delve into four distinct areas where creativity can fuel your entrepreneurial aspirations:

1. **The Innovative Queen:** Thinking outside the box to create new opportunities

2. **The Artistic Queen:** Incorporating creativity into your business and life

3. **The Expressive Queen:** Communicating your vision and ideas effectively

4. **The Inspiring Queen:** Using creativity to inspire and motivate others

By embracing these four aspects of creative energy, you can unlock new levels of success and accomplishment in your business and personal life. Creativity is not merely a talent possessed by artists and writers but a powerful force that can drive growth, transformation, and innovation in any sphere of life.

The Innovative Queen calls upon you to break free from conventional thinking and explore new ideas, opportunities, and possibilities. By embracing an open mindset, you can uncover untapped potential and develop groundbreaking solutions to the challenges you face in your entrepreneurial journey.

The Artistic Queen encourages you to weave creativity into every aspect of your life, from business strategies to personal growth. By nurturing your artistic instincts, you can cultivate a deep sense of fulfillment and passion that will propel you forward on your path to success.

The Expressive Queen emphasizes the importance of clear, compelling communication in conveying your vision and ideas to others. By mastering the art of expression, you can connect with your audience, build lasting relationships, and inspire those around you to join you in your mission.

Finally, The Inspiring Queen urges you to use your creativity to uplift and motivate others, igniting their passion and fostering a collaborative, supportive environment. By harnessing the power of inspiration, you can galvanize your team, customers, and community, creating a ripple effect that extends far beyond your immediate sphere of influence.

As we explore the creative essence of a queen in this chapter, we will weave together the lessons gleaned from the lives of Nefertiti and Maya Angelou, two women who harnessed their creativity to shape the world around them. Through their stories, we will discover how you can tap into your creative power to forge a successful, fulfilling path in business and life.

In the upcoming sections, we will delve deep into the facets of creativity that made these women iconic figures, and we will provide actionable steps you can take to unlock your creative potential. By the end of this chapter, you will have a newfound understanding of the power of creativity and the tools you need to harness it in your entrepreneurial journey.

With the stage set, we invite you to embark on this journey of discovery, embracing your inner Nefertiti and Maya Angelou as you explore the boundless potential of your own creative spirit. Let us now delve into the heart of creativity, beginning with the first aspect: The Innovative Queen.

Imagine a world where you can break free from the confines of conventional thinking and unleash your creativity to shatter the glass ceiling and redefine the limits of possibility. This is the realm of the Innovative Queen, where transformational ideas are born, and boundaries are merely stepping stones on the path to greatness. Are you ready to embrace your inner Innovative Queen and unlock a world of untapped potential? If so, let's embark on this extraordinary journey together.

The Innovative Queen: Thinking Outside the Box to Create New Opportunities

In the realm of the Innovative Queen, conventional wisdom is challenged, and the status quo is defied. This is where creativity and innovation become the driving forces behind groundbreaking ideas, pushing the boundaries of what is possible and redefining the landscape of entrepreneurship.

To truly harness the power of innovation, it is essential to cultivate a mindset that embraces new ideas, seeks out fresh perspectives, and thrives on exploration and experimentation. This can be daunting, particularly in a world that often clings to tradition and resists change. But the rewards can be truly transformative for those who dare to venture beyond the familiar.

So, how can you tap into your inner Innovative Queen and unlock the creative potential that lies within you? Here are some key strategies to help you think outside the box and create new opportunities for yourself and your business.

Embrace a growth mindset: The first step to becoming an Innovative Queen is to adopt a growth mindset, which is the belief that your abilities and intelligence can be developed through dedication and hard work. This mindset encourages you to embrace challenges, persevere through obstacles, and view setbacks as opportunities for growth and learning. By cultivating a growth mindset, you will be better equipped to push beyond your comfort zone, explore new ideas, and take risks that can lead to innovation and success.

Challenge assumptions and question the status quo: Innovative Queens need to be content to accept things as they are. Instead, they continually question the status quo, challenging assumptions and seeking new perspectives. By asking questions and examining your industry's underlying beliefs, you can uncover hidden opportunities and identify areas where change and innovation are needed. Be prepared to challenge conventional wisdom and consider alternative approaches that others may have overlooked or dismissed.

1. **Create a culture of innovation:** As an entrepreneur, you have the power to shape the culture of your business. By fostering a culture that embraces innovation and encourages creativity, you can create an environment where your team feels empowered to share ideas and collaborate on new projects. This can be achieved by celebrating success, embracing failure as a learning opportunity, and providing the resources and support needed to nurture innovation. Encourage open communication and collaboration, and create opportunities for your team to learn, grow, and experiment with new ideas.

2. **Diversify your sources of inspiration:** The most innovative ideas often emerge when diverse perspectives are brought together. By surrounding yourself with people who have different backgrounds, expe-

riences, and expertise, you can gain fresh insights and spark creative thinking. Network with professionals from various industries, attend conferences and workshops, and converse with people who challenge your thinking. Additionally, seek out books, articles, podcasts, and other sources of information that expose you to new ideas and perspectives.

3. **Cultivate curiosity and embrace experimentation:** Innovative Queens are endlessly curious, always seeking to learn and explore new ideas. By cultivating curiosity and embracing experimentation, you can foster a mindset that thrives on discovery and is open to change. Be willing to try new approaches, pivot when necessary, and adapt your strategies based on the results of your experiments. Remember that innovation is an iterative process and that success often comes through failures and lessons learned.

4. **Collaborate with others:** Innovation is rarely a solitary pursuit. By collaborating with others, you can tap into a wealth of knowledge, expertise, and creativity that can fuel your own innovative thinking. Seek partners, mentors, and team members who share your passion for innovation and are willing to challenge your ideas and contribute their perspectives. Be open to feedback and be prepared to revise your statements based on the insights and suggestions of others.

As you embrace these strategies and unlock your inner Innovative Queen, you will find that the possibilities for growth and success are virtually limitless. By thinking outside the box and pushing the boundaries of what is possible, you can create new opportunities for yourself and your business and leave a lasting impact on the world.

With determination, courage, and a willingness to embrace the unknown, you can channel the spirit of Queen Nefertiti and become a true Innovative Queen in your own right.

In the realm of the Artistic Queen, creativity and expression reign supreme. Discover how to infuse your business and life with the power of artistry, transforming the ordinary into the extraordinary and leaving an indelible mark on the hearts and minds of those you encounter.

The Artistic Queen: Incorporating Creativity Into Your Business and Life

Creativity is essential to any successful endeavor and the lifeblood of innovation. In entrepreneurship, harnessing the power of imagination can mean the difference between mediocrity and extraordinary success. By cultivating an environment that nurtures and supports creative thinking, you can elevate your business and personal life to new heights while expanding your horizons and developing a more profound sense of purpose and fulfillment.

The Artistic Queen understands that the power of creativity lies not only in its ability to generate new ideas but also in its capacity to transform the mundane into the extraordinary. By embracing creativity and fostering a culture of imagination and inspiration, you can unlock the door to limitless possibilities and reshape the world around you in profound and meaningful ways.

1. Explore your passions and interests.

One of the most effective ways to ignite your creative spark is to delve into your passions and interests. Whether painting, photography, music, or writing, immersing yourself in activities that bring you joy and fulfillment can help you tap into your inner wellspring of creativity.

By exploring new hobbies and interests, you can expose yourself to fresh perspectives and ideas, which can, in turn, inspire you to think more creatively in your business and personal life. Furthermore, nurturing your artistic side can profoundly impact your overall sense of well-being and happiness, as engaging in creative pursuits has been shown to boost mood, reduce stress, and improve mental health.

2. Cultivate an environment that encourages creativity.

To foster a culture of creativity, creating an environment that supports and nurtures imaginative thinking is essential. This can be achieved by surrounding yourself with inspirational artwork, books, and music and seeking out like-minded individuals who share your passion for creativity and self-expression.

By curating a physical and emotional space that encourages creative exploration and risk-taking, you can unlock your full potential as an entrepreneur and a human being. Furthermore, embracing an atmosphere of collaboration and open-mindedness can inspire those around you to think more expansively and challenge the status quo.

3. Challenge your assumptions and beliefs.

A crucial aspect of cultivating creativity is the willingness to challenge your assumptions and beliefs. This can be accomplished by examining the underlying paradigms that govern your thinking and behavior and questioning whether they truly serve your best interests.

By engaging in critical self-reflection and seeking out alternative perspectives, you can break free from the constraints of conventional wisdom and develop a more expansive, innovative mindset. This process of self-discovery and growth can help you unlock new creative possibilities and become a more empathetic, compassionate, and effective leader.

4. Embrace failure as an opportunity for growth.

One of the most valuable lessons that the Artistic Queen can teach us is embracing failure as an opportunity for growth and learning. By recognizing that failure is an essential part of the creative process, you can develop a more resilient, adaptable mindset and cultivate the courage to take risks and push the boundaries of what is possible.

Rather than viewing failure as a sign of weakness or incompetence, the Artistic Queen sees it as a catalyst for growth and transformation. Reframing failure as a learning opportunity allows you to develop the grit and determination necessary to persevere in adversity and ultimately achieve your goals and dreams.

5. Find inspiration in unexpected places.

The Artistic Queen knows that inspiration can strike at any moment and often in unexpected places. By maintaining a sense of curiosity and wonder, you can open yourself to the myriad creative possibilities around you.

Whether it's a conversation with a stranger, a beautiful sunset, or an evocative piece of music, the world is teeming with potential sources of inspiration. By remaining receptive to the beauty and wonder of the world, you can cultivate a mindset primed for creative breakthroughs and innovation.

6. Share your creative work with others.

Finally, the Artistic Queen understands the value of sharing her creative work with others. By sharing your art, ideas, and innovations with the world, you can inspire others, spark meaningful conversations, and impact your community.

In addition, the process of sharing your work can lead to valuable feedback and insights, helping you refine your craft and further develop your creative skills. You can create a more fulfilling, authentic, and impactful life by embracing vulnerability and connecting with others through your creative expression.

By incorporating these principles into your business and personal life, you can unleash the power of your inner Artistic Queen and create a legacy of creativity, innovation, and success. Remember that the journey of self-discovery and growth is a lifelong process and that by embracing your creative potential, you can transform your own life and those around you.

Are you ready to embark on the path of the Artistic Queen and embrace the transformative power of creativity? In the next section, we'll delve into the world of the Expressive Queen and explore how you can effectively communicate your vision and ideas to inspire, motivate, and empower those around you.

The Artistic Queen has laid the foundation for a life full of creativity and innovation. Now, it's time to amplify your impact by stepping into the shoes of the Expressive Queen. Discover how to effectively communicate your vision and ideas, fostering an environment where creativity flourishes and propels you toward unimaginable success.

The Expressive Queen: Communicating Your Vision and Ideas Effectively

The Expressive Queen understands that the power of creativity and innovation lies in generating new ideas and effectively communicating these ideas to others. To bring your vision to life and inspire those around you, you must develop strong communication skills and become adept at conveying your thoughts with clarity and conviction.

In this section, we'll explore the fundamental principles of effective communication and how you can apply these principles to share your vision, ideas, and creative projects with the world.

1. Clarity is king

The first and most important principle of effective communication is clarity. The Expressive Queen knows that to inspire others and convey the essence of her ideas, she must ensure that her message is clear and easy to understand. This means choosing the right words, using simple and concise language, and avoiding jargon or overly complex terms that may confuse or alienate her audience.

To enhance clarity in your communication, consider the following tips:

- **Use clear and concise language:** Choose simple words and phrases that accurately convey your message, and avoid using jargon or overly complex terms.

- **Be specific:** When discussing your ideas or vision, provide concrete examples and details to help your audience understand the scope and implications of your message.

- **Structure your thoughts:** Organize your ideas logically, and use clear transitions to guide your audience through your narrative.

2. Know your audience

To communicate effectively, the Expressive Queen must understand her audience and tailor her message accordingly. By considering your audience's needs, preferences, and values, you can craft a message that resonates with them and inspires them to take action.

Before you share your ideas, take the time to research and analyze your audience. Consider their background, interests, and potential concerns, and adjust your message and communication style to align with their needs and preferences.

3. Engage your audience with storytelling.

One of the most powerful tools in the Expressive Queen's arsenal is storytelling. By sharing your ideas and vision through stories, you can create an emotional connection with your audience, making your message more memorable and impactful.

To incorporate storytelling into your communication, consider the following tips:

- **Use vivid imagery and sensory details:** Help your audience visualize your ideas by using descriptive language and painting a vivid picture of the scenarios you're discussing.

- **Share personal anecdotes:** Connect with your audience on a deeper level by sharing personal stories and experiences that demonstrate the impact of your ideas.

- **Create a compelling narrative:** Structure your story with a clear beginning, middle, and end, and use conflict and resolution to keep your audience engaged and invested in the outcome.

4. Harness the power of non-verbal communication.

The Expressive Queen understands that effective communication goes beyond words. Nonverbal cues, such as body language, facial expressions, and tone of voice, can significantly impact how your audience receives and interprets your message.

To enhance your nonverbal communication skills, consider the following tips:

- **Maintain eye contact:** Establish a connection with your audience by looking them in the eye while you speak.

- **Use confident body language:** Stand tall, with your shoulders back and your chest open, to convey confidence and authority.

- **Modulate your tone and pace:** Adjust your speech's tone, volume, and pace to convey emotion and emphasize key points.

5. Listen actively and empathetically.

Finally, the Expressive Queen recognizes that effective communication is a two-way street. To truly connect with your audience and understand their needs, you must be willing to listen actively and empathetically, demonstrating genuine interest in their thoughts and concerns.

To improve your listening skills, consider the following tips:

- **Give your full attention:** Focus on the speaker and avoid distractions, such as checking your phone or looking around the room.

- **Ask open-ended questions:** Encourage the speaker to elaborate on their thoughts by asking questions that require more than a simple "yes" or "no" answer.

- **Reflect and paraphrase:** Summarize and rephrase the speaker's main points to demonstrate your understanding and clarify potential misunderstandings.

- **Validate their emotions:** Acknowledge and validate the speaker's feelings, even if you don't necessarily agree with their perspective.

By honing your communication skills and becoming an Expressive Queen, you can effectively share your creative vision and ideas with the world, inspiring others to join you on your journey of innovation and discovery. Through straightforward, engaging storytelling and empathetic listening, you'll foster deeper connections with your audience and unlock the full potential of your creative endeavors.

As we venture into the realm of inspiration, it's time to delve into the essence of being an Inspiring Queen. Discover the secrets to unleashing your creative power and learn how to kindle the flames of motivation in others, sparking a revolution of innovation and success. Are you ready to ignite the world with your passion and vision? Let's begin!

The Inspiring Queen: Using creativity to inspire and motivate others

Unleashing the full potential of your creative genius is a journey that transcends the boundaries of your own world. As an Inspiring Queen, your ability to inspire and motivate others can lead to a powerful ripple effect, spreading your message and influence far and wide. But how can you harness your creativity to uplift those around you and spark a movement of innovation and success? In this section, we'll explore the key strategies and techniques that can help you become a beacon of inspiration for others.

1. Be Authentic and True to Yourself

Authenticity is the cornerstone of inspiration. People are drawn to those who are genuine, open, and honest in their pursuits. Embrace your unique qualities, talents, and experiences, and share them unabashedly with the world. Be transparent about your journey, your struggles, and your triumphs. Doing so creates a space for others to connect with you on a deeper level, allowing them to see themselves in your story and draw strength from your resilience.

2. Cultivate a Positive and Growth-Oriented Mindset

Your attitude and mindset are crucial in your ability to inspire others. Adopt a growth-oriented mindset that embraces challenges, welcomes feedback, and views setbacks as opportunities to learn and grow. Encourage those around you to adopt a similar mindset by sharing your experiences, insights, and lessons learned along your creative journey. By fostering a positive, growth-oriented environment, you can inspire others to push past their boundaries and reach for the stars.

3. Share Your Knowledge and Expertise

Inspiration often begins with a spark of knowledge or a newfound skill. As an expert in your field, you have a wealth of information and experience to share with others. Offer guidance, mentorship, and support to those eager to learn and grow. By generously sharing your expertise, you empower others to pursue their own creative endeavors and establish yourself as a trusted authority and leader in your niche.

4. Encourage Collaboration and Community

Innovation thrives in an environment of collaboration and camaraderie. Create opportunities for others to come together and share their unique perspectives, ideas, and talents. Host workshops, networking events, or brainstorming sessions encouraging open dialogue and creative exploration. By fostering a strong sense of community, you can inspire others to contribute their insights and expertise, leading to a collective pool of knowledge and resources that fuels even greater innovation.

5. Celebrate the Success of Others

As an Inspiring Queen, it's essential to recognize and celebrate the achievements of those around you. By acknowledging the hard work and accomplishments of others, you boost their confidence and motivation and create a culture of support and encouragement. Share the success stories of your peers, team members, or clients, and highlight the valuable lessons that can be learned from their experiences.

6. Lead by Example

Inspiration is best demonstrated through action. Show others what's possible by fearlessly pursuing your dreams and pushing your creative potential's boundaries. Embrace challenges, take risks, and continually strive for improvement. As you pave the way for your own success, you'll inspire others to follow in your footsteps and chase after their own creative aspirations.

7. Communicate Your Vision

Your ability to inspire others hinges on communicating your vision clearly and passionately. Paint a vivid picture of your goals and aspirations, using evocative language and storytelling to convey the essence of your message. Speak from the heart and let your enthusiasm shine through. When your audience can see, feel, and believe in your vision, they'll be inspired to join you on your journey to greatness.

In conclusion, becoming an Inspiring Queen is about tapping into the boundless well of creativity within you and using it to uplift and motivate others. It's about embracing your unique strengths, sharing your expertise, and leading by example to spark a movement of innovation and success. By cultivating a positive mindset, fostering collaboration, and communicating your vision with passion and conviction, you can become a beacon of inspiration for all those around you.

As you embark on this journey, remember the lessons from Queen Nefertiti, who used her innovative spirit and artistic talent to inspire her people and leave a lasting legacy. Channel the wisdom of Maya Angelou, who showed the world that creativity can be a powerful force for change and empowerment. By embodying these qualities and following the strategies outlined in this section, you, too, can become an Inspiring Queen and make a lasting impact on the world around you.

Now that we've covered the four key aspects of being a creative and influential queen, it's time to reflect on your journey and how to implement these principles in your life. Consider the areas where you excel and the areas where you may need to grow. With dedication, practice, and an open heart, you can unleash the full potential of your creative spirit and inspire others to do the same.

And as you embark on this transformative journey, remember you are never alone. In the words of Maya Angelou, "You may encounter many defeats, but you must not be defeated. In fact, it may be necessary to encounter the defeats to know who you are, what you can rise from, and how you can still come out of it."

Are you ready to embrace your inner Inspiring Queen and share your unique gifts with the world? If so, the time is now. Let your creativity shine, and your inspiration guide you to new heights of success and fulfillment.

In conclusion, becoming a Creative Queen requires embracing your innate creativity, thinking outside the box, communicating effectively, and inspiring others through your actions and vision. By drawing inspiration from the lives and lessons of Queen Nefertiti and Maya Angelou, you can cultivate a creative mindset and use it to enrich your personal and professional life.

To help you on your journey, here are five actionable steps to guide you:

1. **Embrace your creativity:** Begin by acknowledging your creative talents and allowing yourself to explore and develop them further. This might involve taking up a new hobby, attending workshops, or simply dedicating daily time to practice and hone your craft.

2. **Think outside the box:** Challenge yourself to approach

problems and situations from new perspectives. Consider alternative solutions, and don't be afraid to take risks or try something unconventional. The more you push your boundaries, the more innovative and resourceful you'll become.

3. **Communicate effectively:** Learn to express your ideas and vision clearly and persuasively, whether through writing, speaking, or other forms of communication. Actively listen to others and engage in meaningful conversations, fostering collaboration and open-mindedness.

4. **Inspire and motivate others:** Share your passion, knowledge, and enthusiasm with those around you and encourage them to explore their creative potential. Be a role model and lead by example, showing others the power of creativity and its ability to transform lives.

5. **Reflect and grow:** Regularly assess your progress and identify areas to improve. Embrace setbacks and failures as opportunities for growth and learning, and continue to evolve as an individual and a Creative Queen.

As you embark on this journey, remember to be patient and kind to yourself. Growth takes time, and self-discovery is an ongoing process. Keep in mind the following mantra as you embrace your inner Creative Queen:

"I am a wellspring of creativity, inspiration, and innovation. I have the power to shape my world and inspire those around me. I am a Creative Queen, and my journey is just beginning."

May this mantra constantly remind you of your potential and the transformative power of creativity. Now go forth and let your inner Creative Queen shine!

Chapter Six

THe communication of a queen

The Power of Royal Communication

ONCE, A WOMAN RULED her empire with a queen's grace and a seasoned leader's wisdom. Queen Nefertiti, an influential figure in ancient Egypt, displayed exceptional communication skills that allowed her to lead and inspire her people effectively. Her story mirrors women's struggles and triumphs in modern-day America, where determination and persistence are necessary to create a lasting impact. Like Nefertiti, we, too, can harness the power of communication to lead and inspire those around us.

Michelle Obama, a modern-day queen in her own right, has also made waves with her powerful speeches. Her words have transcended political boundaries, inspiring people from all walks of life to work together for a common goal. The impact of her words serves as a testament to the power of communication in shaping our world.

In this chapter, we'll explore the key communication qualities that define queens like Nefertiti and Michelle Obama. We'll delve into:

1. Communicating with authenticity and transparency

2. Developing strong communication skills

3. Building effective partnerships and teams

4. Using communication to inspire action and change

These principles will help you become the Unstoppable Woman you were born to be. Let's dive in.

The Authentic Queen: Communicating with Authenticity and Transparency

As an Unstoppable Woman, your words should reflect your true self. In the world of business, authenticity and transparency are invaluable. When you're genuine in your communication, people will feel more connected to you and trust in your leadership.

To be an authentic communicator, understand your values, beliefs, and passions. When you know yourself deeply, you can express your ideas clearly and with conviction. Be vulnerable and open, sharing your experiences and emotions with your audience. This vulnerability fosters trust and strengthens relationships, both personally and professionally.

Here are some ways to communicate with authenticity and transparency:

1. **Share your story:** Your journey, successes, and failures are powerful tools to inspire others. Feel free to share your personal story and the lessons you've learned.

2. **Be present:** When you're engaged in conversation, give the other person your full attention. Listen actively and respond thoughtfully, showing you genuinely care about their thoughts and feelings.

3. **Practice empathy:** Put yourself in the shoes of your audience. Try to understand their emotions, needs, and desires, and adjust your communication style to meet them where they are.

4. **Be honest:** Speak the truth, even when it's uncomfortable or challenging. Honesty is the cornerstone of trust, and people will respect you more.

The Articulate Queen: Developing Strong Communication Skills

Effective communication is an art form that takes practice to master. To be an articulate queen, you must be able to convey your thoughts and ideas with clarity, persuasiveness, and confidence. Strong communication skills will help you navigate personal and professional relationships, empowering you to quickly build your empire.

To develop strong communication skills, consider the following tips:

1. **Use precise language:** Speak concisely and avoid jargon. Keep your message simple and straightforward so your audience can easily understand your point.

2. **Listen actively:** Great communicators are also great listeners. Pay attention to what others are saying and respond thoughtfully. This not only shows respect but also helps you gather valuable information.

3. **Practice non-verbal communication:** Your body language, facial expressions, and tone of voice are crucial in conveying your message. Be aware of these non-verbal cues and use them to reinforce your

words.

4. **Ask for feedback:** Solicit feedback from trusted friends, colleagues, or mentors to identify areas where you can improve your communication skills.

5. **Embrace storytelling:** Stories capture people's attention and make your message more relatable. Use anecdotes and personal experiences to illustrate your points, making your communication more engaging and memorable.

6. **Adapt to your audience:** Different situations call for different communication styles. Learn to tailor your message and delivery to suit your audience, whether you're speaking to a team member, a client, or an investor.

As you develop your communication skills, remember that practice makes perfect. Seek opportunities to hone your abilities, whether through public speaking engagements, networking events, or simply engaging in conversations with others. Over time, you'll become more comfortable and confident in your communication, helping you to connect with others and achieve your goals.

In Section 3, we'll explore the power of collaboration and how your communication prowess can elevate your team to extraordinary heights. It's time to become the Collaborative Queen who unites and empowers her empire.

The Collaborative Queen: Building Effective Partnerships and Teams

Collaboration is the key to success in any venture, and as an Unstoppable Woman, you must cultivate the ability to unite and empower those around you. When you harness the power of collaboration, you can overcome challenges, innovate, and achieve your goals more effectively. Effective communication lies at the heart of collaboration, and as a Collaborative Queen, you'll lead your team to greatness.

Here are some strategies to help you build effective partnerships and teams through solid communication:

1. **Establish a clear vision and goals:** As a leader, it's essential to communicate a clear vision and set achievable goals for your team. This gives them direction and helps them understand how their contributions fit the larger picture. When everyone is aligned, your team can work more effectively to achieve your objectives.

2. **Create an open and inclusive environment:** Encourage open dialogue and create a space where everyone

feels comfortable sharing their ideas, opinions, and concerns. Foster a culture of trust and respect where team members feel valued and heard. This will boost morale and lead to better decision-making and problem-solving.

3. **Encourage diverse perspectives:** Embrace your team members' unique experiences and viewpoints. Diverse perspectives often lead to innovative solutions and ideas you may not have considered otherwise. Encourage your team to challenge assumptions, think outside the box, and be open to their input.

4. **Develop active listening skills:** To be an effective collaborator, you must be an active listener. Pay attention to what your team members say, and avoid interrupting or imposing your ideas on them. You can foster stronger connections and enhance collaboration by showing empathy and understanding.

5. **Provide constructive feedback:** As a leader, it's your responsibility to help your team grow and improve. Offer timely, constructive feedback that focuses on specific behaviors and their impact. Remember to balance your criticism with praise and recognition for a well-done job.

6. **Resolve conflicts constructively:** Disagreements and disputes are inevitable in any team, but how you handle

them can make all the difference. Address conflicts promptly and openly, facilitating a respectful discussion on finding a solution. Encourage your team members to express their concerns and work together to reach a mutually beneficial resolution.

7. **Delegate and empower:** Empower your team by delegating tasks and responsibilities based on their strengths and interests. Trust your team members to take ownership of their work and give them the autonomy to make decisions and solve problems. This boosts their confidence and helps them develop new skills and grow as professionals.

8. **Celebrate successes together:** Recognize and celebrate your team's achievements, both big and small. Acknowledging their hard work and contributions fosters a sense of pride and motivates them to continue giving their best. Celebrating successes together also strengthens the bond within your team, creating a more cohesive and collaborative environment.

By implementing these strategies and leveraging your communication skills, you can foster a collaborative and high-performing team to support you in building your unstoppable empire. Remember, as the Collaborative Queen, your role is to unite, empower, and inspire your team to reach their full potential. Together, you'll achieve great heights and redefine the meaning of success.

As a Collaborative Queen, you have laid the foundation for a thriving, unstoppable team. The next step is to harness the full potential of your communication skills to inspire action and drive change. Section 4 will delve into using your words to ignite passion, create momentum, and inspire those around you to join your mission. Get ready to become the Inspiring Queen who leads her empire to greatness.

The Inspiring Queen: Using Communication to Inspire Action and Change

As an Unstoppable Woman, your ability to inspire others is one of your most powerful tools. Communicating with passion and conviction can ignite change, motivate action, and lead your team toward a brighter future. This section will explore the art of inspiring communication, helping you become the Inspiring Queen who leads her empire to greatness.

Here are some strategies for using communication to inspire action and change:

1. **Speak with passion:** To inspire others, you must first be passionate about your mission, your goals, and the change you want to create. When you speak from

the heart, your enthusiasm and energy will be contagious, motivating those around you to join your cause.

2. **Craft a compelling narrative:** Stories can move people and create lasting connections. To inspire your audience, share personal stories and anecdotes that illustrate your message. You can make your message more relatable, memorable, and impactful by weaving a compelling narrative.

3. **Use powerful language:** Your chosen words can significantly influence how your message is received. Use powerful, evocative language to paint a vivid picture of the future you envision and the impact of the change you seek. This will help your audience understand the importance of your mission and feel inspired to take action.

4. **Engage your audience:** To inspire change, you must connect with your audience on a deeper level. Encourage participation, ask thought-provoking questions, and create opportunities for dialogue. Engaging your audience can foster a sense of ownership and investment in your mission.

5. **Be a role model:** Actions speak louder than words. To inspire your team, lead by example, and demonstrate the values and behaviors you wish to see in others. When you embody the change you seek, you'll in-

spire those around you to do the same.

6. **Set clear expectations and support:** To inspire action, provide your team with clear expectations and the support they need to succeed. Offer guidance, resources, and encouragement, empowering them to take ownership of their work and achieve their goals.

7. **Recognize and reward progress:** Celebrate the achievements and improvement of your team, both big and small. Acknowledging their hard work and contributions will boost morale, motivate continued action, and inspire them to strive for greater heights.

8. **Foster a growth mindset:** Encourage your team to embrace challenges and view setbacks as opportunities for growth. Cultivating a growth mindset inspires resilience, persistence, and a commitment to continuous improvement.

By incorporating these strategies into your communication, you'll become the Inspiring Queen who leads her empire to greatness. With your words, you'll ignite passion, create momentum, and drive your team to achieve their full potential.

As an Inspiring Queen, your communication will motivate your team and create a ripple effect, inspiring others to join your cause and support your mission. Your words can change the world, one conversation at a time.

As we conclude our journey, it's time to reflect on the powerful communication strategies you've learned and how they can transform your life and business. In the final section, we'll recap the key takeaways and provide actionable steps to help you apply these techniques, ensuring you become the Unstoppable Woman who builds a lasting legacy of empowerment and success.

Conclusion

Throughout this chapter, we've explored the importance of effective communication in your journey as an Unstoppable Woman. We've examined various strategies and techniques to help you become the Authentic, Articulate, Collaborative, and Inspiring Queen you were meant to be. As we conclude, let's summarize the key takeaways and provide actionable steps to implement these powerful communication strategies in your life and business.

The Authentic Queen: Communicate with authenticity and transparency by staying true to your core values, being honest with yourself and others, and owning your strengths and weaknesses.

1. **Action step:** Reflect on your values and ensure your communication aligns with them. Practice vulnerability by sharing your authentic self with others.

- **The Articulate Queen:** Develop strong communication skills by embracing storytelling, adapting to your audience, and continually seeking opportunities to practice and refine your abilities.

2. **Action step:** Identify areas where you'd like to improve your communication skills and seek opportunities to practice, such as public speaking engagements or networking events.

- **The Collaborative Queen:** Build effective partnerships and teams by establishing a clear vision, creating an open and inclusive environment, and fostering trust and respect among your team members.

3. **Action step:** Evaluate your current team dynamics and identify areas for improvement. Implement strategies for fostering collaboration and open communication within your team.

- **The Inspiring Queen:** Use communication to inspire action and change by speaking passionately, crafting compelling narratives, and leading by example.

4. **Action step:** Develop a powerful personal story that illustrates your mission and the change you seek. Share this story with others to inspire action and create a ripple effect of change.

As you embark on your journey to becoming an Unstoppable Woman, remember that your communication skills are vital in achieving success and inspiring others to join your cause. Keep refining these skills and apply the strategies and techniques discussed in this chapter to unlock your full potential and build a lasting legacy of empowerment and success.

Before we part, let's end with a powerful mantra to remind you of the Unstoppable Woman you are:

> "I am an Unstoppable Woman, and my words can ignite change, inspire action, and create a lasting impact. I will harness my communication skills to lead, empower, and transform the world around me."

Repeat this mantra daily as a reminder of your power, potential, and the incredible impact you can make through effective communication.

Chapter Seven

THE GROWTH OF A QUEEN

Embracing Evolution

THE SUN BARELY ROSE when I received a phone call that changed everything. One of my most loyal and dedicated employees, Sarah, had just informed me that she was leaving the company. The news hit me like a ton of bricks. She had been my right-hand woman, confidante, and support system in the business world. Her departure left me feeling vulnerable and uncertain about the future of my company.

I knew I couldn't let this setback deter me from my goals. I decided to use this as a catalyst for growth and transformation. I needed to learn how to adapt, to become more resilient, and to embrace the changes life had in store for me.

Through sheer determination, I embarked on a journey of self-discovery and growth that would lead me to become the unstoppable queen I am today. I realized every challenge I faced was an opportunity to learn, grow, and become a more decisive, capable leader.

My journey began with embracing the importance of continuous learning. I knew that to succeed in the ever-changing world of entrepreneurship, I needed to be well-versed in the latest industry trends, technologies, and strategies. I devoured books, attended workshops and seminars, and sought mentorship from those who had achieved the success I aspired to.

As I embraced the role of the Learning Queen, I discovered that my newfound knowledge and skills had a profound impact on my business. I was able to make better decisions, create innovative solutions to challenges, and inspire my team to strive for greatness. The more I learned, the more confident I became in my leadership and entrepreneurial abilities.

The next step in my journey was becoming the Adaptable Queen. The business world is constantly changing, and I realized that I needed to adapt quickly to new circumstances to thrive. I learned the importance of being proactive, anticipating changes, and adjusting my strategies accordingly.

I became a student of change, studying how other successful entrepreneurs had navigated the unpredictable business landscape. I learned to embrace change as an opportunity for growth rather than a threat to my success. With each new challenge, I became more flexible, adaptable, and prepared for the future.

One such challenge came in the form of a global pandemic. The COVID-19 crisis shook the world to its core, forcing businesses to adapt or perish. I knew that to survive, I needed to find innovative ways to serve my clients and community while keeping my team safe and healthy. This required a massive shift in how we operated, but through resilience and adaptability, we survived and thrived.

As I continued to grow and evolve, I discovered the power of being a Visionary Queen. I learned the importance of looking beyond the present, anticipating future trends, and capitalizing on opportunities before they became mainstream. By staying ahead of the curve, I was able to position my business for success in a rapidly changing world.

I began to study market trends, analyze consumer behavior, and monitor technological advancements. I surrounded myself with other visionaries, learning from their insights and experiences. I sought new opportunities, taking calculated risks to propel my business to new heights.

The culmination of my journey was becoming the Innovative Queen. I realized that I needed to constantly innovate and develop new products, services, and business models to sustain growth and achieve lasting success. Innovation became the lifeblood of my company, fueling our growth and setting us apart from the competition.

I fostered a culture of innovation within my team, encouraging them to think outside the box and challenge the status quo. Together, we developed groundbreaking solutions to problems our clients faced, revolutionizing how we did business and positioning ourselves as industry leaders.

Through trial and error, we learned the importance of iterating on our ideas, refining them based on feedback, and continually striving for improvement. We celebrated our successes, but more importantly, we embraced our failures as valuable learning experiences. This mindset allowed us to constantly push the boundaries of what was possible and to stay at the forefront of our industry.

Reflecting on my journey, I realized that becoming an unstoppable queen took work. It was filled with setbacks, obstacles, and moments of doubt. But through perseverance, resilience, and a commitment to growth, I emerged stronger, more capable, and more determined than ever to achieve my goals.

I share my story not to boast about my accomplishments but to inspire you, my fellow queens, to embrace your own journey of growth and transformation. To show you that no matter your challenges, you can rise above them and achieve greatness.

In this chapter, we will explore the four key aspects of growth that every unstoppable queen must embrace:

1. **The Learning Queen:** Continuing to learn and grow as a leader

2. **The Adaptable Queen:** Embracing change and adapting to new circumstances

3. **The Visionary Queen:** Anticipating future trends and opportunities

4. **The Innovative Queen:** Developing new products, services, and business models to fuel growth

By understanding and integrating these principles into your own life and business, you can unlock your true potential and create a lasting legacy of success, empowerment, and inspiration for others.

In Section 1, we will delve into the world of the Learning Queen, uncovering the secrets to harnessing the power of knowledge and education to propel you towards success. Are you ready to embark on a journey of continuous growth and become the unstoppable force you were always meant to be? Let's begin.

The Learning Queen - Continuing to Learn and Grow as a Leader

The Learning Queen is a force to be reckoned with, for she understands that knowledge is power. She knows that to become genuinely unstoppable, she must commit to lifelong learning, growth, and self-improvement. In this ever-changing world, it is crucial to keep up with the latest trends and developments in your industry, as well as to hone your skills and expand your knowledge base. You can only stay ahead of the competition and reach your full potential.

Adopting a growth mindset is the first step to becoming a Learning Queen. A growth mindset is the belief that your abilities and intelligence can be developed through dedication and hard work. This mindset encourages you to embrace challenges, persevere through obstacles, and view failures as opportunities to learn and grow. Here are some strategies to help you cultivate a growth mindset and become a true Learning Queen:

1. **Embrace challenges:** Seek out opportunities to push yourself beyond your comfort zone, whether it's taking on a challenging project at work, learning a

new skill, or pursuing a personal goal. By embracing challenges, you'll develop resilience and adaptability, critical traits of a successful entrepreneur.

2. **Reflect on your failures:** Don't be afraid to fail. Instead, view failures as valuable learning experiences that can help you grow and improve. Reflect on what went wrong and what you can do differently next time, and apply those lessons to future endeavors.

3. **Seek feedback:** Solicit feedback from your peers, mentors, and employees, and be open to constructive criticism. Use this feedback to identify areas for improvement and implement changes accordingly.

4. **Surround yourself with like-minded individuals:** Surround yourself with other ambitious, growth-oriented individuals who share your commitment to self-improvement. These individuals can provide support, encouragement, and inspiration, helping you stay motivated to become an unstoppable queen.

Next, the Learning Queen must commit to ongoing professional development. This can take many forms, from attending workshops and conferences to enrolling in formal education programs. Here are some tips to help you prioritize and make the most of your professional development opportunities:

1. **Set clear goals:** Identify your short-term and long-term professional development goals and create a plan to achieve them. This will help you stay focused and motivated as you pursue your educational and training objectives.

2. **Prioritize relevant opportunities:** There are countless professional development opportunities available, but not all will be relevant to your industry or career goals. Be selective and prioritize those opportunities that will have the most significant impact on your growth and success.

3. **Stay current on industry trends:** Stay informed about the latest trends, developments, and best practices in your industry by reading trade publications, attending conferences, and participating in industry forums and online communities.

4. **Invest in yourself:** Recognize the value of investing in your personal and professional growth and allocate time and resources accordingly. This may mean setting aside weekly time to focus on your development or budgeting for workshops and courses.

Lastly, the Learning Queen must embrace the power of mentorship. Mentorship is a powerful tool that can provide guidance, support, and encouragement as you navigate the challenges and opportunities of entrepreneurship. Here are some tips for finding and working with a mentor:

1. **Identify potential mentors:** Look for individuals who have experience and expertise in your industry and those who share your values and aspirations. These individuals can offer invaluable insights and advice based on their own experiences.

2. **Establish clear expectations:** Discuss your goals and expectations with your mentor, and be open to their feedback and guidance. This will help ensure that both parties are on the same page and can work together effectively.

3. **Be proactive and engaged:** Take the initiative to ask questions, seek advice, and share your challenges and successes with your mentor. Remember, a mentorship relationship is a two-way street, and it's up to you to make the most of it.

4. **Show gratitude and appreciation:** Express your appreciation for your mentor's time, support, and guidance, and demonstrate your commitment to applying their advice and learning from their expertise.

By cultivating a growth mindset, prioritizing professional development, and embracing the power of mentorship, you will be well on your way to becoming the unstoppable

Learning Queen. This commitment to continuous growth and self-improvement will enhance your skills and knowledge and inspire those around you, creating a ripple effect that benefits your entire team and organization.

As a Learning Queen, you'll be better equipped to overcome obstacles, adapt to change, and seize new opportunities. Your dedication to personal and professional growth will serve as a shining example to others, demonstrating that success is not a destination but a journey of constant learning and development.

With a strong foundation as a Learning Queen, you'll be ready to tackle the next challenge to becoming an unstoppable entrepreneur: embracing change and adapting to new circumstances. Stay tuned for Section 2, where we will explore the world of the Adaptable Queen and discover the secrets to thriving in an ever-changing business landscape.

In conclusion, becoming a Learning Queen requires continuous growth and self-improvement. By cultivating a growth mindset, prioritizing professional development, and embracing the power of mentorship, you will be well on your way to becoming an unstoppable force in entrepreneurship. Embrace the journey, for it is through learning and growth that we unlock our true potential and achieve greatness.

Are you ready to dive into the ever-evolving world of business and emerge as a triumphant force? Section 2 will unveil the secrets of the Adaptable Queen, empowering you to thrive in the face of change and seize opportunities others may overlook. Get ready to embrace your inner chameleon and transform challenges into your most significant victories.

The Adaptable Queen

Change is the only constant in the world of business. Your ability to adapt and evolve as an entrepreneur will be the key to your success in an ever-changing landscape. In this section, we will explore the mindset and strategies of the Adaptable Queen, revealing how you can survive and thrive in the face of change.

1. **Embrace a flexible mindset:** The first step to becoming an Adaptable Queen is recognizing that change is inevitable and often beyond our control. By cultivating a relaxed mindset, you'll be better equipped to navigate uncertainty, adjust your plans, and seize new opportunities. Remember, it's not the strongest or the most intelligent who survive but those most adaptable to change.

2. **Stay informed and anticipate change:** To adapt effectively, you must be aware of the changes happen-

ing in your industry, market, and the broader business landscape. Make it a habit to regularly read industry news, attend conferences and networking events, and converse with fellow entrepreneurs, experts, and mentors. You'll be better positioned to anticipate change and adjust your strategies by staying informed.

3. **Develop a solid organizational culture:** A company's ability to adapt to change is directly tied to its corporate culture. Cultivate a culture that values innovation, collaboration, and continuous improvement, and create an environment where employees feel empowered to take risks and contribute their ideas. Encourage open communication and feedback, and provide the resources and support necessary for your team to embrace change and adapt.

4. **Be agile and responsive:** Agility is critical in today's fast-paced business environment. Adopt a lean and flexible approach to business operations, and be prepared to pivot your strategies and tactics as needed. This might involve reevaluating your product or service offerings, exploring new markets, or adjusting your marketing and sales strategies. In the face of change, the key is to be responsive and proactive rather than reactive.

5. **Foster a strong network:** Building a solid network of professional connections is essential for any en-

trepreneur, but it's vital for the Adaptable Queen. Your network can provide invaluable insights, support, and resources as you navigate change and may even present new opportunities for collaboration and growth. Cultivate relationships with fellow entrepreneurs, industry experts, mentors, and potential partners, and be open to learning from their experiences and perspectives.

6. **Learn from setbacks and failures:** Change often brings challenges and setbacks, but viewing these as opportunities for learning and growth is crucial. Embrace a growth mindset, and approach setbacks and failures as valuable lessons to help you adapt and improve. Reflect on your experiences, identify areas for improvement, and apply these learnings to your future endeavors.

7. **Develop resilience:** Resilience is the ability to bounce back from adversity and continue progressing despite setbacks and challenges. To cultivate resilience, focus on building emotional intelligence, practicing self-compassion, and maintaining a strong support network. By developing resilience, you'll be better equipped to navigate change and emerge even stronger on the other side.

In conclusion, becoming an Adaptable Queen requires a flexible mindset, a commitment to continuous learning and improvement, and the ability to navigate uncertainty with resilience and grace. By embracing these qualities and strategies, you will be well on your way to building a sustainable and thriving business in an ever-changing world. Remember, the most successful entrepreneurs are not those who resist change but those who adapt and evolve, seizing new opportunities and transforming challenges into victories.

Are you ready to take your entrepreneurial journey to unprecedented heights? In Section 3, we will unveil the strategies of the Visionary Queen, empowering you to anticipate future trends and position yourself ahead of the curve. Prepare to embrace your inner vision and unlock the potential to revolutionize your industry, leaving a lasting impact on the world.

The Visionary Queen

A true entrepreneur is a visionary who can anticipate future trends, seize untapped opportunities, and create innovative solutions that redefine the marketplace. As a Visionary Queen, your ability to envision the future and take bold, strategic steps toward your goals will set you apart from the competition and position you for unparalleled success. In this section, we will explore the mindset and strategies of the Visionary Queen, empowering you to transform your dreams into reality and leave a lasting impact on the world.

1. Cultivate a forward-thinking mindset: To become a Visionary Queen, you must train your mind to think beyond the present and envision future possibilities. This requires curiosity, creativity, and an unwavering belief in your ability to shape the world around you. Embrace a growth mindset, continually seek new knowledge and experiences, and challenge yourself to imagine the world as it could be rather than accept it as it is.

2. Study trends and emerging technologies: Stay informed about your industry's latest trends and emerging technologies and the broader business landscape. This will help you anticipate future opportunities and disruptions, enabling you to position yourself and your business at the forefront of innovation. Attend industry conferences, read trade publications, and converse with experts and thought leaders to stay abreast of the latest developments.

3. Develop a clear vision and mission: A compelling vision and mission will serve as the foundation for your entrepreneurial journey, guiding your decisions and inspiring others to pursue your goals. Take the time to articulate a clear and inspiring vision for your business, and craft a mission statement that reflects

your core values and purpose. Communicate your vision and mission to your team, partners, and stakeholders, and ensure they align with your strategic objectives.

4. Embrace risk and uncertainty: Visionary leaders recognize that bold, innovative ideas often involve risk and uncertainty. To succeed as a Visionary Queen, you must be willing to take calculated risks and embrace the possibility of failure as an opportunity for learning and growth. Develop a strong risk management strategy, and be prepared to adjust your plans and pivot as needed in response to changing circumstances.

5. Build a culture of innovation: Encourage a culture of innovation within your organization by fostering an environment where creativity, collaboration, and continuous improvement are valued and rewarded. Provide the resources and support necessary for your team to experiment with new ideas and encourage open communication and feedback. Recognize and celebrate successes and embrace a growth mindset that views setbacks and failures as opportunities for learning and growth.

6. Foster strategic partnerships and alliances: Collaborating with like-minded entrepreneurs, experts, and organizations can help you amplify your impact and accelerate your progress toward your goals. Seek out

strategic partnerships and alliances that align with your vision and mission, and explore opportunities for co-creation, joint ventures, and other collaborative initiatives.

7. Stay focused and disciplined: As a Visionary Queen, it's essential to maintain focus and discipline as you work toward your long-term objectives. Develop a strategic plan that outlines your goals, priorities, and key milestones, and regularly review your progress to ensure that you remain on track. Be prepared to make tough decisions and prioritize your time and resources effectively, even when faced with competing demands and distractions.

In conclusion, the Visionary Queen embodies the spirit of entrepreneurship by anticipating future trends, embracing innovation, and taking bold, strategic steps toward her goals. By cultivating a forward-thinking mindset, staying informed about emerging trends and technologies, and fostering a culture of innovation within your organization, you can unlock your full potential as a visionary leader and create a lasting legacy that inspires others to pursue their dreams. Remember, the future belongs to those who dare to envision it, and the most successful entrepreneurs are those who dare to go for it.

The path to exponential growth is paved with innovation. In Section 4, we will delve into the realm of the Innovative Queen, where creativity and boldness merge to create novel solutions that disrupt the status quo. Ready to shape the future of your industry? Let's dive in and discover the strategies that will help you think outside the box, break the mold, and redefine what's possible in your entrepreneurial journey.

The Innovative Queen - Creating Value Through Breakthrough Ideas

The Innovative Queen reigns supreme in a realm where creativity meets execution. Her crown is adorned with gems of ingenuity, and her scepter wields the power of transformative solutions. In a world where many follow trends, the Innovative Queen sets them. She wants more from the status quo; she challenges it, seeking new ways to redefine success, provide value, and elevate her empire.

1. **Cultivate a Problem-solving Mindset:** The first step to innovation is understanding that solutions arise from problems. Embrace challenges as they come, viewing them not as setbacks but as opportunities to innovate. For every problem you encounter, there's a potential breakthrough waiting to be discovered.

2. **Collaborate Widely:** The Innovative Queen understands that innovation doesn't happen in isolation. Surround yourself with a diverse team with varied backgrounds and skill sets. Invite ideas, encourage brainstorming sessions, and welcome suggestions from every corner. Often, the most revolutionary ideas come from the most unexpected places.

3. **Prioritize Research and Development RD:** Allocate resources, both time and budget, towards RD. It's essential to stay ahead, experimenting with new concepts, testing them, and refining them. Foster an environment where experimentation is celebrated and failure is merely a stepping stone toward a groundbreaking solution.

4. **Stay Open to External Innovations:** Not all innovation needs to be in-house. Sometimes, the best ideas or technologies come from outside your company. Being open to partnerships, mergers, or acquisitions might provide the innovative edge you're seeking.

5. **Iterate and Evolve:** As the market changes, so should your products and services. Continuous feedback loops with your customers and stakeholders can provide insights into areas of improvement. Always be prepared to evolve your offerings based on feedback and changing market dynamics.

6. **Stay True to Your Vision:** While innovation requires

adaptability, ensuring that any new direction aligns with the company's core values and vision is essential. It's easy to be swayed by the allure of a new trend, but true innovation aligns novelty with authenticity.

7. **Celebrate Creative Risk-taking:** Encourage your team to take calculated risks. Celebrate those who think outside the box, even if every idea doesn't come to fruition. The culture of valuing effort over outcome can lead to a hotbed of innovative thinking.

In the heart of the Innovative Queen lies a passion for betterment not just for her business but for her customers and the world. She understands that innovation isn't about reinventing the wheel but making it roll smoother, faster, and more efficiently. It's about finding and bridging gaps in the marketplace, seeing possibilities before others do, and having the courage to transform vision into reality.

Your journey as an Innovative Queen will be fraught with uncertainties but remember: every significant change in the world was once an idea in someone's mind. Embrace the challenge, foster a culture of creativity, and continue pushing the boundaries. In the vast business empire, may you rule as the Innovative Queen, leaving a legacy of transformative solutions and groundbreaking ideas.

As we transition from the Innovative Queen to our concluding reflections, remember that innovation isn't a destination; it's a continuous journey. The landscapes of business and technology are ever-evolving, and so should you. Stay curious, stay fearless, and above all, stay innovative.

Conclusion and Action Steps

As we conclude this chapter, we reflect upon the journey you have embarked upon as an entrepreneur. You have risen to the role of the Learning Queen, the Adaptable Queen, the Visionary Queen, and now, the Innovative Queen. Each persona embodies an essential quality of successful entrepreneurship: the thirst for knowledge, the ability to adapt, the foresight to anticipate, and the audacity to innovate.

Remember, innovation is not merely about inventing something new; it's about creating value, improving lives, and positively impacting your industry and community. As an Innovative Queen, you stand at the helm of this transformative journey, shaping your destiny with your vision, creativity, and courage.

Now, let's outline the action steps that will guide you in embracing the Innovative Queen within you:

1. **Develop an innovative mindset:** Start with self-reflection. Challenge your beliefs and assumptions about your

business and industry. Cultivate curiosity, embrace uncertainties, and view problems as opportunities for innovation. Make it a daily practice to think outside the box and push the boundaries of your creativity.

2. **Embed innovation into your company culture:** Organize brainstorming sessions, workshops, or innovation labs to encourage your team to think creatively and share their ideas. Celebrate innovative ideas, reward creative problem-solving, and promote a culture where failure is seen as an essential step in innovation.

3. **Invest in continuous learning:** Allocate a portion of your time and budget for learning and development activities. This could include attending webinars, workshops, conferences or enrolling in online courses. Encourage your team to do the same and share their learnings with the rest of the organization.

4. **Seek diverse collaborations:** Look for opportunities to collaborate with individuals or organizations from different industries or backgrounds. Attend networking events, join industry forums, or participate in cross-industry associations to gain fresh perspectives and stimulate innovative thinking.

5. **Prototype and iterate:** When you have a new idea, put it into action before it is perfect. Develop a proto-

type, test it, gather feedback, and iterate. Repeat this process until you have a product or service that meets your customers' needs and exceeds their expectations.

6. **Protect your innovations:** Consult a legal professional to understand your options for protecting your intellectual property. This could include filing for patents, trademarks, or copyrights, depending on the nature of your innovation.

7. **Measure your innovation efforts:** Develop metrics that reflect the impact of your innovation efforts on your business. Regularly review these metrics and use them to guide your innovation strategy and decisions.

Let's close this chapter with a mantra, a potent reminder of your potential and purpose as an Innovative Queen. Repeat this mantra to yourself, and let it guide you as you navigate your entrepreneurial journey:

"I am an Innovative Queen. I challenge the status quo, disrupt the ordinary, and shape the future with creativity and courage. I turn ideas into value and value into impact. I am not just an entrepreneur; I am a change-maker, a pioneer, a creator. I embrace my potential, and I let my innovative spirit shine."

With these action steps and your mantra, you are well-equipped to embrace the Innovative Queen within you. Remember, your journey as an entrepreneur is not just about building a successful business; it's about redefining success on your terms, creating value, and making a positive impact. Embrace your potential, let your innovative spirit shine, and lead your business toward growth and success.

Chapter Eight

The Legacy of a Queen

Carving Your Royal Legacy

SOME NAMES ECHO THROUGH the corridors of time, leaving an indelible mark on the fabric of history. One such name is that of Queen Nefertiti. In her time, she was a beacon of strength and change, a matriarch who left a legacy that would reverberate through the centuries. As an entrepreneur, I've always been drawn to such stories of strength and resilience. But when I faced my own challenges, I truly understood the depth of her influence.

At a point in my career, I realized I was building an empire but not a legacy. My business was thriving, but it was dependent on me. I constantly juggled responsibilities, leaving no time for personal growth or to give back to my community.

I was successful, but I needed to make a difference. I knew I needed to make a change.

I took inspiration from Queen Nefertiti, who didn't just rule; she transformed. She influenced her time's art, religion, and politics, leaving a lasting impact that is still studied today. So, I shifted my focus from just profit to impact. I implemented strategies to make my business more self-sustaining, invested in my team, and started initiatives to give back to my community. Slowly, I saw the change. I was not just an entrepreneur anymore but a leader leaving a legacy.

This transition was not unlike the journey of another queen of our time, Ruth Bader Ginsburg. A true trailblazer, Ginsburg redefined gender equality and civil rights, leaving a legacy that inspires millions.

In this chapter, we will explore the journey to leaving a legacy, a journey every woman entrepreneur can undertake. We will delve into four key aspects - giving back to your community, creating a lasting impact, inspiring future generations, and using your success to empower others.

The Generous Queen: Giving Back to Your Community and Society

As successful entrepreneurs, we often become so engrossed in our businesses that we overlook our broader responsibilities. Our enterprises, no matter how profitable or groundbreaking, must serve a higher purpose, and that purpose is often deeply intertwined with the society and community that surrounds us.

Let's turn our gaze back to the past. Queen Nefertiti was not only an influential monarch but also a benevolent one. She ensured that her subjects were cared for, their needs met, and their voices heard. This wasn't a duty she performed out of obligation but out of a profound sense of responsibility towards her people. This sense of duty and the willingness to give back differentiates a leader from a ruler.

In the modern entrepreneurial landscape, we can see this mirrored in the endeavors of numerous successful women entrepreneurs. An excellent example is Sara Blakely, the founder of Spanx. Sara has always been vocal about her responsibility to give back. She established the Sara Blakely Foundation, aimed at helping women through education and entrepreneurial training. This initiative has bolstered her personal brand and contributed to a more significant societal cause, building a legacy that extends far beyond her profitable enterprise.

Giving back to the community isn't just about philanthropy or charity. It's about building an ecosystem that nurtures and supports growth, progress, and mutual success. It's about recognizing that our success as entrepreneurs is not isolated from the community we live in, but rather, it's deeply embedded within it.

I FACED MANY CHALLENGES when I started my initiative to give back to my community. The most significant was identifying where my efforts would make the most impact. After careful consideration and research, I decided to support women's education and entrepreneurship, areas close to my heart. I launched scholarships and mentorship programs and provided resources to help budding women entrepreneurs. The positive feedback and success stories I received from these initiatives have been more rewarding than any business accolade.

To honestly give back, we need to engage with our community actively. It could be by mentoring young entrepreneurs, donating to a local charity, sponsoring community events, or using our platforms to advocate for causes we believe in. The key is identifying a cause that aligns with your values and business ethics.

As entrepreneurs, we can use our resources, influence, and platforms to create meaningful change. Investing in our communities contributes to societal development and cultivating an environment that fosters mutual growth, innovation, and progress. It's about creating a ripple effect of positive change that will continue to impact lives long after we're gone.

This is the mark of a generous queen - a woman who understands her success is intertwined with the success of her community, a woman who uses her power and influence to uplift those around her. By giving back, we're building a legacy for ourselves and paving the way for future generations of women entrepreneurs to thrive and succeed.

As we continue our journey, we'll delve into the realm of visionaries-those who dared to dream, innovate, and disrupt the status quo. They didn't just build businesses; they transformed industries and left an indelible mark on the world. Are you ready to embrace your inner vision and create a lasting impact through your business and leadership?

The Visionary Queen: Creating a Lasting Impact Through Your Business and Leadership

In entrepreneurship, some merely exist, and then there are the visionaries. The visionaries are the game-changers who disrupt industries, challenge the status quo, and leave a legacy transcending time. They are the women like Oprah Winfrey, synonymous with transformation and resilience.

Oprah Winfrey's story is a testament to the power of vision. Born into poverty in rural Mississippi, she faced numerous challenges and adversities in her early life. However, she refused to be defined by her circumstances. Instead, she chose to rise above them, driven by an unwavering belief in her potential and a clear vision of what she wanted to achieve.

When Oprah entered the media industry, she was among the few women and even fewer people of color. Yet, she navigated this male-dominated industry gracefully and became the first African-American woman to host a nationally syndicated talk show. The Oprah Winfrey Show wasn't just a talk show; it was a platform that sparked conversations, inspired change, and touched lives across the globe.

Oprah's vision extended beyond the realm of television. She founded Harpo Productions and the Oprah Winfrey Network, further cementing her position as a powerful force in media. She used her influence to spotlight societal issues, support education, and promote diversity and inclusion.

Reflect on Oprah's journey and the legacy she continues to build. It's not just about the wealth she has accumulated or the awards she has won. Oprah's real impact lies in the lives she has touched, the conversations she has started, and the doors she has opened for others.

As an entrepreneur, your business is your canvas, and your vision is the masterpiece you create. Your vision differentiates you, drives you, and ultimately defines your legacy. A visionary entrepreneur doesn't just build a successful business; they shape industries, influence trends, and leave a lasting imprint on the world.

Here are some strategies to help you embrace your inner visionary:

1. **Think Big, Start Small:** Visionaries dream big but understand the value of starting small. They know that every outstanding achievement begins with a single step. So, dream big, but also be willing to start where you are with what you have.

2. **Challenge the Status Quo:** Visionaries are fearless in questioning how things are. They challenge existing norms, disrupt complacent industries, and introduce innovative solutions. Be bold and ask, challenge, and disrupt.

3. **Build a Legacy, Not Just a Business:** A visionary's goal is to build a successful business and create a lasting legacy. Consider how your business can create value, contribute to society, and influence future generations.

4. **Stay True to Your Vision:** Visionaries are unwavering in their commitment. They don't let failures deter them or critics dissuade them. Stay true to your vision, even when the road gets tough.

Oprah Winfrey once said, "Create the highest, grandest vision possible for your life because you become what you believe." As a visionary queen, you have the power to create a successful business and a legacy that inspires and impacts generations to come.

The impact of visionary leadership continues beyond industry disruption and legacy creation. It also weaves an inspiring narrative that fuels the dreams and ambitions of future generations. So, as we turn the pages of our entrepreneurial journey, let us step into the shoes of 'The Inspiring Queen,' whose life and work ignite the spark of possibility in the hearts of aspiring entrepreneurs.

The Inspiring Queen: Inspiring Future Generations of Women Entrepreneurs

From the boardrooms of Fortune 500 companies to the buzzing start-up spaces, one name resonates with an unrelenting force, shaping the future of women in business-Indra Nooyi. Former CEO of PepsiCo, Nooyi's journey from her humble beginnings in India to becoming one of the world's most influential business leaders is a testament to her inspiring prowess.

Nooyi never shied away from dreaming big, even when the odds were stacked against her. She worked her way up, armed with an unwavering determination and an unyielding work ethic. Her relentless pursuit of excellence led her to the helm of PepsiCo, where she shattered the glass ceiling, becoming one of the few women to lead a global conglomerate.

Her leadership at PepsiCo was transformative. During her tenure, the company saw an 80 growth in sales, attributed to her strategic redirection of the company's efforts towards healthier products. However, the numbers only tell half the story. Nooyi's impact transcends beyond profit margins and market shares. She emerged as a beacon of hope for every woman who dared to dream big in adversity.

Nooyi's approach to leadership embodied a rare blend of visionary thinking and compassionate empathy. She championed the notion of 'Performance with Purpose,' placing equal emphasis on the bottom line and the well-being of employees, communities, and the environment. Her commitment to creating a more inclusive and diverse corporate world continues to inspire a new generation of women entrepreneurs.

Beyond her corporate achievements, Nooyi was open about balancing her demanding career and personal life. Her candidness about the challenges of working mothers in a high-powered job shed light on the often-overlooked difficulties many women face. By sharing her experiences, she inspired a dialog on work-life balance that continues today, paving the way for more supportive corporate policies.

Just like the inspiring queens of the past, Nooyi utilized her success as a platform to encourage more women to step into leadership roles. She once said, "I wouldn't ask anyone to do anything I wouldn't do myself," a leadership principle she lived by, inspiring her team through actions and not just words. This ethos of leading by example resonates with the new-age entrepreneurs who look up to her.

Indra Nooyi's legacy goes beyond her accomplishments at PepsiCo. Her journey, filled with courage, resilience, and an enduring spirit, is a powerful source of inspiration for millions of aspiring women entrepreneurs. She continues to inspire and empower, proving that with audacity and determination, women can break down barriers and rewrite the game's rules.

Nooyi's story reminds us that as women entrepreneurs, we are building businesses and creating legacies that inspire future generations. The narrative of our journey, the trials we overcome, and the successes we achieve serve as the building blocks for the dreams of those who follow in our footsteps.

To conclude, Indra Nooyi's inspirational journey demonstrates how a woman of grit and determination can reshape the business landscape while inspiring future generations.

Her legacy as an inspiring queen continues to encourage and embolden women entrepreneurs worldwide to break barriers and achieve their dreams.

Imagine a world where every successful woman becomes a catalyst for change, a powerhouse of influence, and a beacon of empowerment for other women and marginalized communities. That is the world we're about to explore in the next section. Stay tuned as we delve into the realm of "The Empowering Queen."

The Empowering Queen: Using Your Success to Empower Other Women and Marginalized Communities

The Empowering Queen is a force to be reckoned with. She doesn't just command respect; she commands transformation. Just as a queen bee has the power to shape the destiny of her hive, the Empowering Queen uses her success to empower other women and marginalized communities, sowing the seeds for a better, more equitable world.

Let's take the case of Melinda Gates, co-founder of the Bill and Melinda Gates Foundation, who stands as a paragon of an Empowering Queen. After achieving tremendous success in her career, Gates turned her attention towards philanthropy, leveraging her wealth and influence to improve education, healthcare, and equality worldwide. Her commitment to empowering women is commendable, with a significant portion of her Foundation's work dedicated to improving women's access to healthcare, education, and financial services.

However, it was only sometimes smooth sailing for Gates. She started her career at Microsoft, leading the corporate ladder in a male-dominated tech industry. Despite the challenges she faced, she remained undeterred. Her determination and resilience earned her a top spot in the company and gave her the platform she needed to pursue her philanthropic endeavors.

When she co-founded the Bill and Melinda Gates Foundation with her then-husband, Bill Gates, she used her success to foster change on a global scale. The Foundation is now one of the world's leading charitable organizations, driving progress in areas like public health, development, and policy advocacy, primarily in low-income countries.

One of the Foundation's core focus areas is gender equality, which Gates believes is the key to solving many of the world's most pressing issues. She has championed initiatives to close the gender gap in technology and politics and has invested heavily in programs supporting women's health and education.

Moreover, Gates has been an outspoken advocate for women's rights. She has utilized her platform to draw attention to issues like gender discrimination and violence against women, urging world leaders to take action. By doing so, she has provided financial support to women and marginalized communities and given them a voice, advocating for their rights and pushing for societal change.

Her empowerment initiatives have had a profound impact, helping countless women access resources and opportunities previously out of reach. Through her work, she has demonstrated that success is not just about accumulating wealth or power; it's about using those resources to make a difference.

Gates' story is a perfect example of how women in business can use their success to empower others. By leveraging her influence and resources, she has driven significant change, improving the lives of millions of women and marginalized individuals worldwide.

This journey towards empowerment is not exclusive to women like Melinda Gates. You, too, can become an Empowering Queen. It starts with understanding the power within you and the ability to transform lives and communities. Remember, every step you take toward success is not just a victory for you; it's a victory for every woman who sees you as a beacon of hope and empowerment.

As we move towards the conclusion of this chapter, let's reiterate our journey through the realm of queens. From the Generous Queen to the visionary, the Inspiring, and now, the Empowering Queen, we've seen how women in business can create a lasting legacy that transcends time and space. Let's bring it together and understand how to apply these lessons to your journey.

Our journey through the realm of queens has been remarkable, full of inspiring tales of women who have made their mark in the business world. As we reach the end of our journey, it's time to reflect on our lessons and look ahead to the path that awaits. How can we channel the spirit of the Generous, Visionary, Inspiring, and Empowering Queens? The answer lies in the conclusion of our tale.

So, you've seen the legacy of a queen, not just in terms of what she builds during her reign, but in the impact she leaves that resonates through generations. The Generous Queen, the Visionary Queen, the Inspiring Queen, and the Empowering Queen embody a unique facet of leadership that we can incorporate into our entrepreneurial ventures.

As a generous queen, I understand the importance of giving back. Your success is not a stand-alone victory but a triumph that can uplift others. Seek ways to contribute to your community, share your resources, and support initiatives that align with your values.

Action Step 1: Identify a cause you are passionate about and devise ways your business can support it, either through direct contributions or by offering your products, services, or time.

As a visionary queen, your role is to leave a lasting impact through your business and leadership. You must anticipate changes, innovate, and adapt, making decisions that will shape a better future for all those touched by your empire.

Action Step 2: Develop a long-term strategic plan for your business that incorporates financial goals and social and environmental impact.

As an inspiring queen, you can motivate future generations of women entrepreneurs. Share your journey, your struggles, and your victories. Let your story be the beacon that guides others on their path.

Action Step 3: Mentor a budding woman entrepreneur or offer internships to young women interested in your industry. Write a blog post or create a video sharing your entrepreneurial journey.

As an empowering queen, you have the potential to transform lives. Use your success to foster an environment of empowerment where women can thrive and reach their highest potential.

Action Step 4: Implement policies in your organization that promote gender equality, such as equal pay, flexible working hours, and opportunities for professional development for women.

Action Step 5: Invest in women-led businesses or become part of networks that provide resources and support to women entrepreneurs.

You become more than a successful businesswoman by weaving these elements into the fabric of your entrepreneurial journey. You become a queen, leaving a legacy that extends far beyond your empire and persists long after your reign.

As we conclude, remember this: Every woman is a queen in her own right, with the power to shape her destiny and the world around her. Every step you take and every decision you make leaves an imprint, forming a legacy that will reverberate through time. Embrace your queenly qualities and let them guide you on your journey.

And as you venture forth, carry this mantra close to your heart,
"I am a queen. I build. I inspire. I empower. My legacy is my strength."

Let this be the guiding principle of your journey, the compass that steers you toward a legacy that truly embodies the spirit of a queen. Let your empire be your masterpiece, a testament to your strength, resilience, and passion. For you are a queen, and your reign is just beginning.

Chapter Nine

THE RITUALS OF A QUEEN

Unveiling the Rituals of a Queen

A RICH TAPESTRY OF life is woven from the threads of daily rituals, each strand a testament to our priorities, values, and the essence of who we truly are. Behind every successful woman is a meticulously curated set of rituals practiced with discipline and grace that is the foundation of her triumphs. In this chapter, I invite you to step into the world of queens, both ancient and modern, to explore the rituals that have been their guiding light.

Just as the sun's daily journey across the sky signifies the passage of time, so do our personal rituals mark the ebb and flow of our lives. I recall a time in my journey when my world seemed shrouded in chaos. As an entrepreneur, wife, and mother, I found myself torn between the demands of my blossoming empire and the intimate whisperings of my home.

Each day felt like a relentless tug-of-war battle between professional aspirations and personal fulfillment. It was then that I realized a crucial truth: the art of balancing lies not in dividing oneself between roles but in integrating all facets of life into a harmonious whole. This revelation led me to explore and ultimately adopt a set of rituals that would breathe rhythm and grace into my everyday life.

The inspiration for this transformative journey came from an unlikely source: the ancient Egyptian queen, Nefertiti. A woman of power and grace, Nefertiti ruled beside her husband, Pharaoh Akhenaten, during a significant cultural and political change in Egypt. Despite the weight of her crown, she was renowned for her poise, charisma, and beauty, which radiated from within.

Historical records and artifacts reveal that Queen Nefertiti upheld a daily routine steeped in mindfulness, gratitude, and self-care. She began her day with an early morning bathing ritual and anointing herself with sacred oils, signifying physical cleansing and spiritual purification. Amidst the demanding responsibilities of her role, she consistently carved out moments of quiet reflection and prayer, a testament to her deep commitment to spiritual growth and well-being.

Inspired by Nefertiti's example, I began incorporating similar practices. I started my mornings with a self-care ritual, setting aside time for meditation, journaling, and gentle exercise. I integrated moments of mindfulness and gratitude throughout my day, pausing to appreciate the beauty around me and savor the joy in even the simplest tasks.

The impact of these rituals was profound. I discovered a wellspring of energy, resilience, and joy within me that fueled my endeavors and enriched my relationships. My business flourished, not at the expense of my personal life, but in harmony with it. I was no longer simply surviving each day; I was thriving, leading with the grace and poise of a queen.

Today, we see reflections of these ancient rituals in the practices of high-achieving individuals. Oprah Winfrey, a queen in her own right, is known for her dedication to mindfulness and meditation. Similarly, Arianna Huffington, co-founder of The Huffington Post, has become a vocal advocate for self-care, sleep, and well-being as pillars of success. Their examples and countless others affirm the timeless wisdom of queenly rituals.

In the sections to follow, we will delve deeper into the rituals of self-care Section 1, gratitude Section 2, mindfulness Section 3, and joy Section 4. Together, we will explore how you, too, can integrate these practices into your life, transforming your everyday routine into the rituals of a queen.

The Self-Care Queen: Prioritizing Self-Care and Well-being

The canvas of our lives is painted with the colors of our daily practices, each hue a testament to our priorities, values, and inherent worth. Among these colors, self-care shines brilliantly, a lustrous gold that infuses our days with radiance and vitality. In queens, self-care is not a luxury but a non-negotiable commitment, an affirmation of their worth, and an investment in their reign.

Every morning, as the first rays of dawn painted the sky, Queen Nefertiti would begin her day with a self-care ritual. Bathing in the sacred waters of the Nile, she would cleanse her body, preparing it for the day ahead. Following this, she would anoint herself with fragrant oils, each with unique healing and protective properties. This ritual was not merely a routine but a sacred practice, an act of reverence towards herself and the divine within her.

Emulating this ancient wisdom, I embarked on my self-care journey. I set aside an hour each morning, dedicating this time solely to nurturing my well-being. This included a blend of physical activities such as yoga and aerobic exercises, mental exercises like meditation and visualization, and emotional practices such as journaling and positive affirmations.

Initially, this was a challenge as I grappled with the guilt of prioritizing myself amidst many professional and personal responsibilities. However, I soon realized that self-care was not a selfish act but rather an act of self-love and respect. By caring for myself, I was better equipped to care for others and handle my responsibilities gracefully and effectively.

The transformation I experienced was profound. My energy levels soared, my mind was more precise, and my emotions more balanced. I became more productive and creative, and my relationships deepened. I felt a new sense of peace and contentment, which I carried throughout the day, coloring my interactions and endeavors with its radiance.

In the fast-paced world of entrepreneurship, it's easy to pay attention to self-care to pursue success. We often prioritize our businesses, clients, and teams at the expense of our well-being. However, this approach could be more sustainable in the long run. Just as a car requires regular maintenance to run smoothly, so do we need to care for our physical, mental, and emotional well-being to perform at our best.

When we embrace self-care, we send a powerful message to ourselves and the world: that we value ourselves, respect our needs, and are worthy of care and attention. We are setting boundaries that protect our time and energy, empowering us to lead with strength and resilience.

Consider Oprah Winfrey, a modern-day queen, who attributes much of her success to her self-care practices. Despite her demanding schedule, she prioritizes daily meditation, exercise, and a healthy diet, practices that nourish her body, mind, and spirit. Her commitment to self-care is a testament to its transformative power and a powerful reminder of its significance in our lives.

Incorporating self-care into our daily routine does not require grand gestures or significant time investment. It could be as simple as taking a few minutes each day to breathe deeply, enjoy a cup of tea, or write in a journal. It could involve setting boundaries around work hours to ensure time for rest and relaxation. It could mean choosing nutritious foods, exercising regularly, or making time for hobbies and activities that bring joy.

Finding practices that resonate with you and fill you with peace, joy, and fulfillment is vital. Remember, this is your journey, and your self-care practices should reflect your unique needs and preferences.

In conclusion, self-care is a powerful tool that can fuel our success, enhance our well-being, and transform our lives. As entrepreneurs, we are the most crucial asset in our businesses, and caring for ourselves should be our top priority.

By adopting self-care practices that nourish our body, mind, and spirit, we can tap into our innate strength and resilience, empowering us to lead with grace, confidence, and vitality.

Remember, self-care is not a one-size-fits-all solution, and what works for one person may not work for another. Experiment with different practices, listen to your body and honor your unique needs. Above all, be patient and compassionate with yourself, for change takes time, and the journey to well-being is a marathon, not a sprint.

Action Steps:

1. Evaluate your current self-care practices. Are they serving your well-being, or do they need a revamp?

2. List activities that bring you joy, peace, and fulfillment. Incorporate at least one into your daily routine.

3. Set boundaries around your work hours to ensure time for rest and relaxation.

4. Prioritize physical activities that you enjoy. Aim for at least 30 minutes of exercise every day.

5. Practice mindfulness. This could involve meditation, deep breathing, or simply being present in the moment.

Having covered the importance of self-care, we now turn our gaze to another powerful practice: cultivating gratitude. Like a soft, gentle rain, gratitude can nourish our spirits, transforming our perspective and enhancing our well-being. Join me in the next section, where we delve into the world of the Grateful Queen, exploring the power of gratitude and how we can integrate it into our lives.

The Grateful Queen: Cultivating Gratitude and Appreciation in Daily Life

As we stride forward on our journey, we now encounter the realm of the Grateful Queen. In this realm, gratitude isn't just an emotion; it's a way of life, a mindset that shifts our perspective from what's lacking to the abundance that's already present in our lives.

In the bustling streets of the entrepreneurial world, it's easy to get caught up in a never-ending cycle of wanting, achieving, and then wanting more. Yet, amidst this whirlwind of aspirations and achievements, the Grateful Queen stands apart. She understands that true success and fulfillment don't merely stem from reaching new heights but appreciating the journey and recognizing the blessings already within her grasp.

I recall an incident that profoundly shaped my understanding of gratitude. I was at a conference in Chicago, feeling overwhelmed and stressed by the demanding schedule, when I ran into an old friend, Lisa. A successful entrepreneur herself, Lisa radiated a sense of calm and contentment that I found contagious. Curious, I asked her what her secret was. She said she starts each day with a warm smile by writing down three things she's grateful for.

Intrigued, I decided to give it a try. Before diving into work, I began writing down three things I was thankful for each morning. Some days, it was as simple as a warm cup of coffee or a phone call with a friend. Other days, it was the achievement of a business milestone or an opportunity to collaborate with someone I admired. This seemingly small practice had a profound impact. I started each day with a positive mindset, focusing on my blessings rather than my challenges, which made my days less stressful and more fulfilling.

Just like Queen Nefertiti, whose appreciation for the beauty and abundance of her kingdom was reflected in her era's flourishing art and culture, we, too, can cultivate a mindset of gratitude that enriches our lives and businesses.

A similar philosophy is adopted by renowned individuals like Oprah Winfrey, who credits her success to her gratitude journal. Arianna Huffington, co-founder of Huffington Post and author of Thrive, also advocates for gratitude, emphasizing that recognizing and appreciating the good in our lives can significantly enhance our overall well-being and success.

Gratitude is not merely an emotion but a skill we can cultivate. Here are some ways we can integrate gratitude into our lives:

1. **Keep a Gratitude Journal:** As I did, start each day by jotting down three things you're grateful for. It could be a person, an experience, a small pleasure, or a significant achievement.

2. **Express Your Gratitude:** Don't just feel grateful, express it. Whether it's thanking a team member for their hard work, showing appreciation for a loved one, or acknowledging a stranger's kindness, expressing gratitude enhances our relationships and spreads positivity.

3. **Gratitude Meditation:** Incorporate gratitude into your mindfulness practice. Focus on something you're grateful for during meditation, and let that appreciation envelop you.

4. **Gratitude Walks:** Take a walk and reflect on your gratitude. This incorporates physical activity into your routine and allows you to connect with nature, enhancing your sense of gratitude.

In conclusion, cultivating gratitude can significantly enhance our well-being, success, and fulfillment. We can navigate our entrepreneurial journey with a positive mindset, resilience, and joy by shifting our focus from lacking to the abundance already present.

Action Steps:

1. Start a gratitude journal and write down three things you're grateful for daily.

2. Express your gratitude. Say thank you to someone who has helped or supported you today. 3. Incorporate gratitude meditation into your mindfulness practice.

3. Take a gratitude walk, reflecting on the things you're thankful for.

4. Cultivate a mindset of gratitude. Remind yourself regularly of the blessings in your life.

When we integrate gratitude into our lives, we enhance our personal well-being and professional success. Gratitude allows us to appreciate our achievements, value our relationships, and maintain a positive attitude amidst challenges, making our entrepreneurial journey more fulfilling and successful.

As we journey forward, we will explore another realm, the realm of the Mindful Queen. A domain where presence is paramount, where each moment is savored, where the hustle and bustle of the entrepreneurial world are tempered by the tranquility of being in the 'now.' The question is, are you ready to step into the shoes of the Mindful Queen? Stay tuned as we unravel the secrets of mindfulness in our next section.

The Mindful Queen: Practicing mindfulness and presence in all activities

In the heart of ancient Egypt, under the reign of Queen Nefertiti, the Nile would flow with a serenity that resonated with her soul. The queen, amidst her imperial duties, would often retreat to the riverbanks, gazing at the undulating waves, sensing the rhythm of the universe in its ceaseless flow. In all its tranquil majesty, the Nile served as a potent symbol of mindfulness for the queen, a reminder to be present and engaged in every moment, to live fully and wholeheartedly, irrespective of the circumstances.

Mindfulness, the practice of being completely present and fully engaged in the current moment, is a potent tool recognized and revered by successful individuals throughout history. Its transformative power lies in its ability to tether us to the 'now,' enabling us to find serenity amidst chaos, clarity amidst confusion, and resilience amidst adversity.

In today's hyper-connected, fast-paced world, entrepreneurs often juggle multiple roles and responsibilities, their minds incessantly flitting between the past and the future, rarely settling in the present. As a result, they may feel overwhelmed, stressed, and disconnected, hindering their personal well-being and professional success.

When I began my entrepreneurial journey, I, too, found myself entangled in the web of constant doing, always planning for the future, seldom present in the moment. My days were filled with meetings, deadlines, and countless tasks, leaving little room for mindfulness. However, over time, I realized the cost of this constant hustle - my health began to deteriorate, my relationships suffered, and my creativity dwindled.

I knew I had to make a change. Inspired by Queen Nefertiti and countless successful individuals who championed mindfulness, such as Oprah Winfrey and Arianna Huffington, I began incorporating mindfulness practices into my daily routine. I started with simple breathing exercises, gradually moving to mindfulness meditation, mindful eating, and even mindful walking. I made it a point to fully immerse myself in whatever task I was doing, whether it was preparing a business proposal or savoring a cup of coffee.

The transformation was profound. Not only did I feel more relaxed and focused, but I also noticed a significant improvement in my productivity, creativity, and decision-making abilities. Mindfulness allowed me to find balance and harmony amidst the chaos of entrepreneurship, fostering resilience, clarity, and well-being.

As entrepreneurs, we can harness the power of mindfulness to enhance our personal well-being and professional success. Whether taking a few minutes daily to meditate, practicing mindful eating, or simply taking a mindful walk in nature, these practices can help us stay grounded, focused, and resilient in our entrepreneurial journey.

Moreover, mindfulness can foster creativity and innovation, essential traits for any entrepreneur. Being fully present opens us to new ideas and perspectives, enhancing our problem-solving abilities and promoting innovative thinking. Arianna Huffington, co-founder of the Huffington Post, aptly puts it, "We think, mistakenly, that success is the result of the amount of time we put in at work, instead of the quality of time we put in."

In the realm of the Mindful Queen, presence is not merely a practice but a way of life, a sacred commitment to live each moment fully and wholeheartedly. The rhythm of the universe, embodied in the undulating waves of the Nile, serves as a constant reminder to be present, to engage fully in each moment, and to embrace the 'now' with openness and curiosity.

As we explore the rituals of a queen, we will delve into the realm of the Joyful Queen, a domain where joy and pleasure infuse every aspect of life.

As we nurture mindfulness, we cultivate a profound sense of peace and harmony that permeates all aspects of our lives. Our relationships deepen, our health improves, and our businesses thrive. We become more responsive and less reactive, more creative and less mechanical, more resilient and less fragile. We evolve into the best version of ourselves, embracing each moment with grace, courage, and authenticity.

And remember, mindfulness is not a destination but a journey. It's not about achieving a state of perpetual calm or eliminating all stress from our lives. It's about embracing each moment, the pleasant and the unpleasant, the mundane and the extraordinary, with openness, curiosity, and kindness. It's about showing up fully for our lives savoring the richness and diversity of our human experience.

In the words of Jon Kabat-Zinn, a renowned mindfulness teacher, "Mindfulness means being awake. It means knowing what you are doing." As entrepreneurs, leaders, and humans, we owe it to ourselves and the world to be awake, know what we are doing, and lead with mindfulness, compassion, and wisdom.

The journey of the mindful queen is a testament to the transformative power of presence, a powerful reminder that the quality of our lives is determined not by the quantity of our achievements but by the quality of our attention. It invites us to awaken from the trance of constant doing, to reclaim our lives from the clutches of busyness, and to embrace the sacredness of the present moment.

Now that we have journeyed through the realms of the Self-Care Queen, the Grateful Queen, and the Mindful Queen, let us venture into the realm of the Joyful Queen. In this realm, joy is not merely an emotion but a state of being, a radiant energy that infuses every aspect of life, fueling our dreams, nurturing our relationships, and empowering us to create a legacy of love, joy, and fulfillment. How does the Joyful Queen find happiness in the everyday? Let's uncover this in the next section.

The Joyful Queen: Finding Joy and Pleasure in Daily Tasks and Activities

Just as a vibrant sunflower turns its face towards the sun, the Joyful Queen turns her face towards joy, choosing to imbue her everyday experiences with delight, wonder, and pleasure. It is not that she is immune to challenges or hardships. Instead, she understands the profound power of joy to heal, transform, and uplift and consciously cultivates it in her daily life.

Consider the story of JK Rowling, the celebrated author of the Harry Potter series. Before her monumental success, Rowling led a life marked by adversity. She was a single mother, living on welfare, struggling to make ends meet. However, she found joy in the act of writing, in the creation of a magical world filled with adventure and mystery. Despite her circumstances, she dedicated time each day to write, often in local cafes, with her baby daughter sleeping beside her.

Rowling has said that she wrote Harry Potter to escape her complicated reality and find joy amid the challenges. And in doing so, she not only transformed her own life but also touched the lives of millions of readers worldwide. Her story is a potent reminder of the transformative power of joy, of the magic that unfolds when we choose to follow our bliss.

The Joyful Queen understands that joy is not merely an emotion to be experienced but a force to be cultivated. She does not wait for joy to arrive; she creates, nurtures, and spreads it. She knows that joy is not found in grand achievements or material possessions but in the simple, ordinary moments of life - in the warmth of the sun on her skin, the aroma of her morning coffee, the sound of her children's laughter, the sight of a blooming flower, the satisfaction of a task well done.

She seeks joy not as an escape from reality but as a pathway to a more profound, prosperous, fulfilling truth. She recognizes that joy is not the absence of pain but the presence of love, gratitude, and company. She embraces joy as her birthright, guiding star, and raison d'tre.

The Joyful Queen is not a Pollyanna, blind to the realities of life. She acknowledges the existence of pain, loss, and hardship, but she chooses not to dwell on them. She decides to focus on the blessings, the opportunities, and the beauty. She prefers to rise above the drama, the negativity, the chaos. She chooses to be the sunshine in her own life and the lives of others.

The Joyful Queen understands that joy is contagious. When she radiates charm, she uplifts those around her, creating a ripple effect of positivity and inspiration. She knows that her happiness can ignite a spark of hope in someone's heart, lighten someone's burden, and brighten someone's day. She chooses to be a beacon of joy in a world that desperately needs it.

She also understands that joy is resilient. It can thrive amid adversity, blossom amid chaos, and shine amid darkness. It is not a fleeting emotion but a steadfast state of being, a deep wellspring of love, hope, and courage. It is her anchor in the storm, her compass in the wilderness, her balm in the battlefield.

The Joyful Queen knows that joy is not a destination but a journey, not an outcome but a process. She savors the journey, cherishes the process, and revels in the adventure. She finds joy not only in the peak but also in the climb, not only in the goal but also in the journey, not only in the destination but also in the journey.

The Joyful Queen lives by the wisdom of the ancient philosopher Epicurus, who said, "Not what we have, but what we enjoy, constitutes our abundance." She measures her success not in material wealth but in joy, fulfillment, and love. She understands that these are the true treasures of life, the real markers of a life well-lived.

She finds joy in the creative process, the act of birthing new ideas, and the thrill of innovation. She finds joy in collaboration, the synergy of minds coming together, and the co-creation of something greater than the sum of its parts. She finds joy in service, the privilege of making a difference, and the honor of contributing to the well-being of others.

The Joyful Queen does not chase happiness; she creates it. She does not seek satisfaction; she cultivates it. She does not wait for fulfillment; she manifests it. She understands that joy is a choice, a commitment, a way of life. She is the architect of her joy, the master of her happiness, the queen of her fulfillment.

As we journey through life, we all have the potential to become Joyful Queens. It is not about denying our challenges or suppressing our pain. It is about focusing on the joy, cultivating gratitude, and embracing the present moment's beauty. It is about choosing to dance in the rain, bloom in the desert, and shine in the darkness. It is about choosing to be the sunshine in our own lives and the lives of others.

The Joyful Queen shows us that joy is not an elusive dream but a tangible reality we can create, nurture, and share. She shows us that joy is not a luxury but a necessity, a powerful catalyst for personal growth, professional success, and social change. She shows us that joy is not a fleeting emotion but a powerful force that can transform our lives, communities, and world.

In the words of the poet Rumi, "Let the beauty of what you love be what you do." Let the joy of what you love be what you do. Let the joy of what you love fuel your journey, the light for your path, the wind for your sails.

As we journey towards becoming Joyful Queens, let us remember the words of the great Maya Angelou, "My mission in life is not merely to survive, but to thrive; and to do so with some passion, some compassion, some humor, and some style." Let us choose to thrive with joy, passion, compassion, humor, and style. Let us choose to be Joyful Queens, living our lives with happiness, spreading joy, and inspiring fun.

We've seen how the daily rituals and practices of Queen Nefertiti contributed to her overall well-being and success. In the next section, we will delve deeper into how we can incorporate these practices into our own lives and become Joyful Queens in our own right.

In this final section, we'll bring together everything we've learned from the life and practices of Queen Nefertiti, the high-achieving individuals of our time, and the four pillars of self-care, gratitude, mindfulness, and joy. We'll look at how we can weave these principles into our daily lives and rise as unstoppable queens, empowered and ready to transform our lives and the world around us. Stay tuned as we begin the journey to manifest our own destiny.

The Unstoppable Queen: Embodying the Rituals of Resilience and Transformation

In the preceding sections, we've journeyed through the sacred rituals of self-care, gratitude, mindfulness, and joy, inspired by the life of Queen Nefertiti and the practices of today's high-achieving women. These rituals serve as guideposts on our path to becoming unstoppable queens women who are successful in their ventures, balanced in their personal lives, resilient in the face of adversity, and empowered to create lasting change in the world.

Let's look at the life of Mary Barra, the CEO of General Motors. Amidst the challenges of leading one of the world's largest automakers, she strongly focuses on her well-being. She makes time for regular exercise, nourishes her body with healthy food, and ensures she has downtime to unwind and rejuvenate. This is a testament to the power of self-care.

Malala Yousafzai, the youngest Nobel Prize laureate, is a beacon of gratitude. Despite her trials, she continuously expresses her appreciation for the support she receives and the opportunities she has been given to make a difference. Her life underscores the transformative power of gratitude.

Indra Nooyi, the former CEO of PepsiCo, practices mindfulness in her daily life. She takes time to reflect on her actions, to be present in her interactions, and to make conscious, thoughtful decisions. Her approach to leadership exemplifies the clarity and focus that comes with mindfulness.

Spanx founder Sara Blakely is a living embodiment of joy. She brings an infectious enthusiasm to her work, celebrates her wins, and even finds humor in her failures. Her journey illustrates how joy can fuel our success and sustain us through the ups and downs of entrepreneurship.

Each of these women showcases a facet of the rituals we've discussed, illuminating the path to becoming an unstoppable queen.

Action Steps:

1. **Prioritize Self-Care:** Schedule time for activities that nourish your body, mind, and soul. Make it non-negotiable, whether it's a workout, a healthy meal, or a relaxing bath.

2. **Cultivate Gratitude:** Start each day by writing down three things you're grateful for. This simple practice can shift your focus to the abundance in your life and fuel your motivation.

3. **Practice Mindfulness:** Be fully present in your activities. Whether working on a project or spending time with loved ones, give your full attention to the moment.

4. **Find Joy Every Day:** Seek out activities that bring you joy. Celebrate your wins, find humor in your challenges, and infuse fun into your daily tasks.

5. **Embody Your Inner Queen:** Embrace the qualities of self-care, gratitude, mindfulness, and joy in your daily life. Remember, you are an unstoppable queen, and these practices will empower you to achieve your goals and leave a lasting legacy.

As we conclude this chapter, let's affirm our commitment to these practices with a powerful mantra:

"I am an unstoppable queen. I honor myself through self-care, enrich my life with gratitude, enhance my presence with mindfulness, and illuminate my journey with joy."

Let this mantra guide you as you navigate your path to success, embodying the rituals of a queen and leading with resilience, grace, and unwavering determination. You are unstoppable. You are a queen. And your empire awaits.

Chapter Ten
THE ABUNDANCE OF A QUEEN

Queen Nefertiti - A Paragon of Abundance

MANY PEOPLE SEE THE world through a lens of scarcity, convinced there's never enough. I was once like this - always chasing after the next big opportunity, fearing that someone else would if I didn't grab it. However, my perspective shifted dramatically when I began to study the life of Queen Nefertiti.

Nefertiti, whose name means "the beautiful one has come," was an Egyptian queen renowned for her beauty and power. But beyond her physical allure, Nefertiti was an embodiment of abundance. She reigned during one of the wealthiest periods in Ancient Egyptian history and used her resources to build a prosperous and culturally rich society.

A personal encounter with scarcity struck me in the early years of building my business. Balancing my personal life and rapidly growing enterprise was a juggling act that left me feeling drained and stretched thin. I was caught in a vortex of ever-increasing demands, and I felt like I was running on a hamster wheel, always busy but not making substantial progress.

This was when I turned to history for wisdom, specifically to Queen Nefertiti. From her, I learned the value of seeing the world through a lens of abundance rather than scarcity. As I studied her life and reign, I was struck by how she leveraged the resources at her disposal to create prosperity for herself and her entire kingdom.

Nefertiti's reign was marked by significant architectural and cultural developments. She didn't hoard her wealth but invested it back into her kingdom, commissioning public works and fostering the arts. This created a flourishing society renowned for its contributions to history and culture.

I took a leap from Nefertiti's book and began approaching my business with an abundance mindset. Instead of fretting over what I lacked, I focused on what I had and how to use it to create more value. I invested in my employees, my business's infrastructure, and partnerships that opened up new opportunities. The results were transformative. My business thrived, and I discovered a newfound sense of fulfillment and balance.

Reflecting on the parallels between my journey and Nefertiti's, I realized that a mindset of abundance goes beyond mere financial prosperity. It's about recognizing the inherent value in ourselves and others and leveraging this value to create a more prosperous and fulfilling life.

In a more recent context, Melinda Gates, co-founder of the Bill Melinda Gates Foundation, embodies a similar spirit of abundance. Her wealth has impacted countless lives through philanthropy, focusing on education, healthcare, and poverty reduction. Her life is a testament to the transformative power of an abundance mindset in the modern world.

As we delve deeper into this chapter, we'll explore how you can cultivate an abundance mindset, build wealth and financial independence, give back to society, and create a legacy of prosperity for future generations. Each element the Abundant Queen, the Wealthy Queen, the Generous Queen, and the Visionary Queen represents a facet of a life lived fully and abundantly.

The journey to abundance begins with a shift in mindset, from scarcity to abundance, from fear to courage, from self-doubt to self-belief. It's a journey I've undertaken and one I invite you to embark on.

Despite life's challenges, we always have the power to choose how we perceive and respond to them. This shift in perspective from scarcity to abundance has the potential to transform not only our lives but also the world around us.

In the following sections of this chapter, we'll delve into the specific strategies that can help you cultivate this mindset and create a life of abundance. You'll learn to become an abundance queen, radiating positivity and attracting prosperity. As a Wealthy Queen, you'll gain the tools to build financial independence. Embracing the spirit of a Generous Queen, you'll discover the joy and fulfillment that comes from giving back. Finally, as a Visionary Queen, you'll learn to create a legacy that continues to generate abundance for future generations.

By the end of this chapter, I hope you see the world through a lens of abundance, just like Queen Nefertiti and Melinda Gates. This shift in perspective is not just about creating financial prosperity. It's about living a rich life in every sense of the word - a life of joy, fulfillment, impact, and legacy.

Action Steps:

1. Reflect on your current mindset. Do you tend to see the world through scarcity or abundance?

2. Read about the lives of Queen Nefertiti and Melinda Gates. What aspects of their approach to abundance resonate with you?

3. Identify one area of your life where you'd like to cultivate more abundance. It could be your career, relationships, personal growth, or any other aspect that feels important to you.

4. Write down three specific actions that you can take to cultivate more abundance in this area.

5. Start taking these actions and observe the changes that unfold in your life.

Abundance is not a destination to arrive at but a journey to embark on. It's a journey that starts with a single step, a single decision to see the world through a lens of plenty rather than scarcity. Are you ready to take this step?

In the next section, we'll delve deeper into the mindset of the Abundant Queen. We'll explore how you can cultivate this mindset, drawing from the wisdom of Queen Nefertiti and other women who have walked this path before us. Are you ready to step into your power and embrace abundance in all its forms?

The Abundant Queen: Cultivating an Abundance Mindset

Imagine Queen Nefertiti standing on her palace balcony, overlooking Amarna's flourishing city. She wasn't born a queen, but her mindset of abundance led her to become one of the most powerful women in history. Nefertiti saw the world not as it was but as it could be. She visualized a prosperous and thriving city and took the necessary steps to manifest this vision.

Abundance begins in the mind. It's not about how much you have but how much you perceive you have. It's about seeing the wealth of opportunities and having the confidence to seize them.

So, how can you cultivate this mindset?

Step 1: Shift Your Focus from Scarcity to Abundance

The first step towards cultivating an abundance mindset is to shift your focus away from scarcity. Instead of dwelling on what you lack, start appreciating what you have. Each morning, write down three things you are grateful for. It could be something as simple as a warm cup of coffee or a kind word from a friend. Over time, this simple practice can help you shift your perspective from scarcity to abundance.

Step 2: Visualize Abundance

Just like Queen Nefertiti, you need to visualize the abundance you desire. Create a vision board that represents your goals and dreams. Each day, spend a few minutes visualizing these goals as if they have already been achieved. Feel the joy, the excitement, the satisfaction. This practice will help align your thoughts and actions toward achieving these goals.

Step 3: Embrace a Growth Mindset

Cultivating an abundance mindset also requires embracing a growth mindset. Believe that you can learn, grow, and improve. Embrace challenges as opportunities for growth. Remember, every setback is a setup for a comeback.

Step 4: Surround Yourself with Positive Influences

Lastly, surround yourself with positive influences. Spend time with people who inspire you, uplift you, and see the world through a lens of abundance. Read books, listen to podcasts, and attend seminars that nourish your mind and spirit with positive, empowering ideas.

Cultivating an abundance mindset isn't a one-time event; it's a journey. It's about making small, consistent shifts in your thoughts and actions. It's about seeing the world through a lens of abundance, even when circumstances seem challenging. It's about embracing your inner Abundant Queen.

In the same way that Queen Nefertiti visualized and brought to life a thriving city, you, too, have the power to create a life of abundance. It all starts with cultivating an abundance mindset.

In the next section, we will explore how to become a Wealthy Queen, harnessing this mindset to build financial independence. We'll delve into strategies and tools you can use to generate wealth and create financial freedom. Are you ready to step into your power and claim your monetary sovereignty?

The Wealthy Queen: Building Wealth and Financial Independence

In the annals of history, Queen Nefertiti is renowned for her beauty and wealth. But her affluence wasn't just about amassing gold and jewels; it was about achieving financial independence that allowed her to rule a kingdom, build a city, and make a lasting impact.

Much like Nefertiti, you can build your wealth and create financial independence. The journey towards financial freedom begins with understanding the principles of wealth creation and implementing them in your life.

Principle 1: Understand the Power of Compound Interest

Albert Einstein once said, "Compound interest is the world's eighth wonder. He who understands it earns it; he who doesn't pays it." Compound interest is the process where your interest on your money also earns interest. Over time, this leads to exponential growth of your wealth. Even a tiny amount, invested wisely and left untouched, can grow into a significant sum.

Principle 2: Diversify Your Investments

The old adage, "Don't put all your eggs in one basket," holds true for building wealth. Diversifying your investments reduces risk and increases potential returns. Consider a mix of stocks, bonds, real estate, and other investment options. Each asset class behaves differently over time, offering a balance between risk and return.

Principle 3: Create Multiple Income Streams

Relying on a single source of income can be risky. Creating multiple income streams provides financial security and accelerates wealth creation. Consider passive income options like rental, dividend, or creating a digital product that generates income even when you're not actively working.

Principle 4: Practice Conscious Spending

Building wealth is not just about how much you earn but how much you save and spend. Be mindful of your spending habits. Avoid impulse purchases and focus on buying assets, not liabilities. Remember, the goal is to accumulate wealth, not possessions.

Principle 5: Invest in Yourself

Lastly, the best investment you can make is in yourself. Enhance your skills, acquire new knowledge, maintain good health, and nurture positive relationships. Your ability to earn, save, and invest depends on your skills, knowledge, health, and network.

Building wealth and achieving financial independence isn't a get-rich-quick scheme; it's a journey that requires knowledge, discipline, and persistence. But the reward of economic freedom the ability to live on your own terms and make choices based on what you truly desire and not merely what you can afford is priceless.

Queen Nefertiti's wealth allowed her to create a thriving city and leave a lasting legacy. Similarly, your wealth can allow you to live your dreams and positively impact the world. You, too, can be a Wealthy Queen.

The following section will explore becoming a Generous Queen, using your wealth to give back to others and contribute to society. We'll delve into the transformative power of generosity and how it can not only change the lives of others but also enrich your own life in profound ways. Are you ready to step into the shoes of the Generous Queen?

The Generous Queen: Giving Back to Others and Contributing to Society

Like the ancient Egyptian Queen Nefertiti, who used her wealth for the welfare of her people, the third step on your journey is about becoming a Generous Queen. But generosity is not just about giving away money; it's about making meaningful contributions to bring about positive societal change.

The Power of Philanthropy

Philanthropy is the desire to promote the welfare of others, expressed primarily by the generous donation of money to good causes. This concept is not new; it has been practiced for centuries by people with the resources to make a difference. From Andrew Carnegie's libraries to Melinda Gates' work in global health and education, philanthropists have left their mark on society.

For a Generous Queen like yourself, philanthropy offers a way to use your wealth for positive change. Donating to causes you care about can help solve societal problems, support those in need, and create a better world for future generations.

Volunteer Your Time and Skills

While monetary contributions can significantly impact society, giving back isn't just about writing checks. You can also donate your time and skills. Volunteer for a local charity, mentor a young person or offer your professional skills to non-profit organizations. Not only does this provide valuable help to those who need it, but it also enriches your life with purpose and fulfillment.

Create a Social Enterprise

Another way to give back is by creating a social enterprise a business that aims to generate profit while solving social problems. A social enterprise could be anything from a fair-trade coffee shop that supports coffee farmers in developing countries to a tech startup that develops affordable healthcare solutions. As a Generous Queen, you can use your entrepreneurial skills to create a business that does well.

Foster a Culture of Giving

As a leader, you can foster a culture of giving in your community, workplace, or family. Encourage others to participate in charitable activities, match their donations, or offer paid volunteer time to your employees. As more people join in, the impact of your generosity multiplies.

Giving with Gratitude

Finally, give with gratitude. Recognize that your ability to provide is a privilege. Be grateful for the opportunities you've had and the resources you can share. This mindset enhances the joy of giving and makes your contributions more meaningful.

Becoming a Generous Queen is a rewarding journey. It's about using your resources money, time, skills, or influence to make a positive difference. Like Queen Nefertiti, who used her wealth to build a thriving city for her people, you too can use your abundance to create a better world.

In your journey's next and final step, you'll become a Visionary Queen, creating a legacy of abundance and prosperity for future generations. You'll learn how to sustain your wealth and generosity, ensuring your impact continues long after your time. Are you ready to take this final step to becoming a Queen of Abundance?

As a Generous Queen, your actions can have a profound and lasting impact. Not only do you have the opportunity to create a ripple effect of positive change, but you also can inspire others to do the same. As you share your abundance, remember to do so with an open heart and gratitude. This attitude will enhance the joy of giving and make your contributions more meaningful.

And so, as we conclude this section, remember that generosity is a choice that comes from within. It's about more than just giving away money or resources; it's about sharing your abundance in a way that contributes positively to society and enriches your life. Your journey to becoming a

Generous Queen is enriching and filled with opportunities to create change and leave a lasting impact.

As we move forward, our journey takes us to a new horizon. In the next section, we will explore the realm of the Visionary Queen. We will delve into how you can create a legacy that extends your abundance and prosperity to future generations. You have generously built wealth and shared it, and now it's time to ensure its sustainability. Are you ready to envision a future where your impact continues to resonate?

The Visionary Queen: Creating a Legacy of Abundance and Prosperity for Future Generations

Once you have established your wealth and embraced the joy of giving, you may ponder what will happen to your hard-earned fortune. As a Visionary Queen, you are not just thinking about the immediate impact of your actions but also the long-term effects. You're not just building for today but for tomorrow, the next generation, and the generations to follow.

Consider the story of Madam C.J. Walker, an African-American entrepreneur, philanthropist, and political activist, who was recorded as the first female self-made millionaire in America by the Guinness Book of World Records. Born to former slaves, she faced numerous challenges in her early life, including poverty, lack of formal education, and racial discrimination. Despite these obstacles, Walker rose to prominence by developing and marketing a successful line of beauty and haircare products for black women through her Madam C.J. Walker Manufacturing Company business.

Madam C.J. Walker was not just content with creating wealth for herself; she was passionate about paving the way for future generations of black women entrepreneurs. She donated substantially to numerous institutions such as the NAACP, the Black YMCA, and other charities. Walker also bequeathed nearly two-thirds of her future net profits to charity in her will.

Just like Walker, as a Visionary Queen, you have the power to ensure your wealth continues to make a difference long after you're gone. This could involve setting up a charitable foundation or trust, investing in businesses and ventures that align with your values and mission, or mentoring and educating younger generations so they can carry your legacy forward.

The first step towards creating a legacy is defining what you want that legacy to be. Do you want to support education, advance science, help the less fortunate, or champion women's rights? Your legacy should be an extension of your passions and values, a testament to the life you've lived.

Next, consider the resources you have at your disposal. Apart from money, think about how your knowledge, skills, and connections could be used to further your cause. For instance, you could establish a scholarship fund, build a school, or create an incubator for women entrepreneurs. Remember, your legacy doesn't have to be grand to be significant; it just needs to reflect your commitment to making a positive impact.

Finally, involve your family and loved ones in your plans. Share your vision with them and inspire them to continue your work. By doing this, you're not just passing on wealth but on values, wisdom, and a spirit of generosity.

In the end, a Visionary Queen knows that true wealth isn't about how much you accumulate but how much of it you can use to enrich the lives of others. She understands that creating a legacy of abundance and prosperity isn't just an act of future planning; it's a lifelong journey of purposeful living.

In the next and final section, we will summarize the lessons from this chapter and provide action steps to guide you on your journey from an Abundant Queen to a Wealthy Queen, a Generous Queen, and ultimately, a Visionary Queen. The future awaits your reign. Are you ready to step up to the throne and craft a legacy that reflects your vision of abundance and prosperity?

As we embark on the final leg of this journey, it's time to look back and absorb the wealth of knowledge we've gathered. Remember, every step you've taken thus far has led you toward becoming the Abundant, Wealthy, Generous, and Visionary Queen you are destined to be. In conclusion, we will bring everything together and provide a roadmap to help you navigate your journey toward building an enduring legacy of abundance and prosperity. But remember, the journey doesn't end here; instead, it's just the beginning. Are you ready to embrace your destiny and make a difference that will echo through generations?

Embrace Your Destiny

After this transformative journey, it's time to pause, reflect, and consolidate the wisdom we have discovered together. The essence of a queen is not defined solely by her crown but by the richness of her spirit, the wealth she amasses not just for herself but for her people, and the legacy she leaves behind.

Look back at the phenomenal women who exemplify this spirit of abundance, wealth, generosity, and vision. Women like Madam C.J. Walker, the first female self-made millionaire in America, used her wealth to enjoy a luxurious lifestyle and empower other women by training them to become beauty consultants, thereby creating a ripple effect of wealth and abundance.

Then there's Sheryl Sandberg, who, despite facing personal tragedy, channeled her resilience and strength into action, advocating for gender equality in the corporate world and mentoring countless women through her initiatives.

Lastly, let's remember Indra Nooyi, former CEO of Pepsi-Co, one of the few women who have reached the highest echelons of the corporate world. She used her position to advocate for healthier products and promote diversity in leadership.

In their unique ways, these women embodied the principles we've explored: cultivating an abundance mindset, building wealth and financial independence, giving back to society, and creating a legacy for future generations. Their lives are testaments to the limitless potential within each of us.

Now it's your turn to step into your power and embrace your destiny. Here are the five action steps to guide you:

1. **Cultivate an abundance mindset:** Start each day with gratitude. Recognize and appreciate the abundance already present in your life. This mindset shift will open you to new opportunities for wealth and prosperity.

2. **Build your wealth:** Educate yourself about financial matters. Seek advice from financial advisors, read books, and attend seminars. Actively work on increasing your income streams and invest wisely.

3. **Give back:** As your wealth grows, remember to give back. This could be through charitable donations, mentoring others, or even starting your foundation. The universe rewards those who help others.

4. **Create your legacy:** Think about the impact you want to leave on the world. What will you be remembered for? Start taking actions today that align with this vision.

5. **Stay resilient:** There will be setbacks and hurdles on this journey. Stay resilient, draw strength from your purpose, and remember that every failure is a stepping stone towards success.

Remember, the journey to becoming an abundant, wealthy, generous, and visionary queen is not a sprint but a marathon. It requires perseverance, resilience, and a burning desire to make a difference.

As we conclude this chapter, I leave you with this mantra,
"I am an abundant, wealthy, generous, and vi-

sionary queen. I create my destiny and build a legacy of abundance and prosperity."

May this mantra guide, strengthen, and inspire you as you embark on this transformative journey. The path is yours to forge, the destiny yours to create. Embrace your power, your potential, and your purpose. Your journey to abundance and prosperity starts now.

Here's an example of a daily worksheet inspired by the action steps in this chapter. This is designed to help you track your progress and make the most of the principles discussed.

Chapter Eleven
THE BALANCE OF A QUEEN

The Resilient Queen

I T WAS A COLD December night, the city lights twinkling below my high-rise office like countless dreams waiting to be realized. I was the last one in the building, once again. Amid the looming deadlines and increasing pressure, I should have noticed the passage of time. Suddenly, the reflection in the glass showed a woman who was successful but also exhausted and isolated. That woman was me.

This was different from the picture of success I had envisioned. I had strived for an empire, and I had built it. Yet, the cost was steep. The balance between my work and personal life had tipped dangerously towards the former, and it was taking its toll.

It was then that I came across the story of Queen Nefertiti, a woman who wielded power and influence in ancient Egypt and yet was revered not just for her leadership but for her ability to maintain harmony and balance in her personal and professional life.

Queen Nefertiti, known for her exquisite beauty and power, was more than a queen. She was a symbol of resilience and balance. She ruled Egypt side by side with her husband, Pharaoh Akhenaten, at a time when women were rarely seen in positions of power. Despite the weight of her responsibilities, she found a way to balance her duty to her people with her role as a wife and mother. In a male-dominated society, she carved a space for herself that allowed her to fulfill her personal and professional roles with grace and dignity.

Her story resonated with me. I realized that I had been so focused on building my empire that I had forgotten to take care of the queen myself. I needed to restore balance to my life.

Drawing inspiration from Queen Nefertiti, I started redefining my success concept. I sought to build a sustainable business without my constant presence. I strived to make time for my personal life and relationships. Slowly but surely, I began to see changes. My stress levels decreased, my relationships improved, and interestingly, my business started to thrive more than ever.

This transformation was not an overnight process but a journey. A journey that was enlightening and empowering. It reminded me of the importance of balance and harmony in life, a lesson I wish to share through this chapter.

This chapter will explore four key aspects that helped me and many successful women leaders, like Indra Nooyi, former CEO of PepsiCo, to achieve this elusive balance.

- **Section 1** will delve into 'The Balanced Queen: Balancing Work and personal life for optimal well-being.' We will explore techniques and strategies that can help you create a harmonious balance between your work and personal life.

- **Section 2** will discuss 'The Harmonious Queen: Cultivating Harmony in Relationships and Work Environments.' Here, we will examine the importance of fostering healthy relationships at work and home and how they contribute to a balanced life.

- **Section 3** will focus on 'The Peaceful Queen: Cultivating inner peace and harmony.' We will explore how inner peace and self-care contribute to balance and well-being.

- **Section 4** will discuss 'The Flexible Queen: Adapting to changing priorities and needs.' We will delve into the importance of flexibility and adaptability in maintaining balance.

Through this chapter, I will guide you on becoming a balanced queen, just like Queen Nefertiti, striking a perfect blend of professional success and personal fulfillment.

The Balanced Queen: Balancing Work and Personal Life for Optimal Well-being

In today's fast-paced world, the quest for work-life balance is more critical than ever. As driven, ambitious women, we are often told that we can "have it all," but the reality of balancing a demanding career with a fulfilling personal life can sometimes feel like an uphill battle.

Looking at the lives of successful women leaders, I found that they often shared a common trait: the ability to maintain a healthy balance between their work and personal lives. For instance, Indra Nooyi, the former CEO of PepsiCo, is a shining example of this. Despite the immense responsibilities of leading a global corporation, she prioritized her family and personal well-being.

So, how can we emulate these successful women and achieve a similar balance in our lives? The journey begins with acknowledging that work-life balance is not a static state but a dynamic process.

Firstly, it is crucial to clearly define what balance means to you. Each person's definition of balance will be different. For some, it might mean spending equal time at work and with family; for others, it might mean dedicating specific days to personal pursuits or setting boundaries between work and personal time.

For example, early in my career, I defined balance as spending equal hours at work and home. However, as my business grew, I realized that the quality of time mattered more than the quantity. I started prioritizing tasks and setting boundaries. I made it a rule not to check emails after 7 p.m. and kept weekends exclusively for personal time. This gave me more time with my loved ones and made me more focused and productive at work.

Secondly, it's essential to regularly check in with yourself. Ask yourself: Am I happy? Do I feel stressed or overwhelmed? Do I have time for activities that I enjoy? Reflecting on these questions can help you understand if your current lifestyle aligns with your idea of balance.

Thirdly, it is essential to prioritize and delegate. As entrepreneurs, we must often be involved in every aspect of our business. However, this can lead to burnout and can negatively impact our personal life.

Take a lesson from successful leaders like Nooyi, who once said, "You cannot have it all." She meant you cannot do everything yourself - you must delegate and rely on a team. After all, one of the key goals of an entrepreneur is to create a business that can run efficiently even when you are not present.

For instance, when I felt overwhelmed with my responsibilities, I started delegating tasks to my team. I hired a competent manager to oversee daily operations, allowing me to focus on strategic planning and decision-making. This reduced my workload and empowered my team, leading to a more productive work environment.

Lastly, it's important to prioritize self-care. Remember, you cannot pour from an empty cup. Regular exercise, a healthy diet, adequate sleep, and hobbies that you enjoy are all critical for maintaining your physical and mental well-being.

In my journey towards achieving balance, I realized the importance of regular exercise. I started practicing yoga and meditation, which improved my physical health and helped me manage stress better. This had a positive impact on both my work and personal life.

Achieving work-life balance is not a destination but a continuous journey of self-discovery, setting boundaries, and making conscious choices. As we move towards creating this balance, we become not just successful entrepreneurs but also happier, more fulfilled individuals.

Section 2 will delve into an equally crucial aspect of balance: cultivating harmony in relationships and work environments. Remember, harmony doesn't just happen; it's a melody we consciously compose. Whether it's a symphony or cacophony depends on the notes we choose to play. The question is, are you ready to be the maestro of your own orchestra?

The Harmonious Queen: Cultivating Harmony in Relationships and Work Environments

Maintaining harmony in relationships and work environments is vital for personal and professional growth. A harmonious work-life ecosystem can lead to exceptional outcomes, just as a well-conducted orchestra creates beautiful symphonies. Here are some strategies to help you cultivate harmony in your relationships and work environments:

1. **Communication:** The foundation of any relationship is open, honest communication. This applies to both personal and professional relationships. Encourage open dialogue, actively listen to others' perspectives, and be willing to share your thoughts and feelings. This creates an environment of trust and understanding.

For instance, I make it a point in my business to have regular one-on-one meetings with my team members. These meetings provide a platform for discussing work progress, addressing concerns, and sharing ideas. This open communication fosters a sense of trust and respect among team members, leading to a more harmonious work environment.

2. **Emotional Intelligence:** Emotional intelligence is the ability to understand, manage, and express your emotions, as well as empathize with others. Developing emotional intelligence can help you navigate relationships and work environments more efficiently. Practice empathy, manage your feelings, and be aware of how your actions impact others.

I recall a situation where one of my team members struggled to meet deadlines. Instead of reprimanding them, I approached the problem with empathy and understanding. I discovered they were facing personal issues that affected their work performance. By offering support and flexibility, I helped them overcome their challenges, leading to improved performance and a more harmonious work environment.

3. **Establishing Boundaries:** Setting boundaries is crucial for maintaining harmony in personal and professional relationships. Be clear about your expectations and communicate them effectively. This can help prevent misunderstandings and conflicts.

For example, I have established a boundary between my work and personal life by not checking work emails after a specific time. This practice has improved my work-life balance and set an example for my team, creating an atmosphere where everyone respects each other's personal time.

5. **Conflict Resolution:** Conflicts are inevitable in any relationship or work environment. How you handle these conflicts can significantly impact harmony. Approach conflicts with a problem-solving mindset, focus on finding solutions and avoid blame.

In my experience, addressing conflicts head-on and involving all relevant parties in the resolution process has proven effective. Conflicts can often be resolved quickly and amicably by creating an environment where everyone feels heard and respected.

6. **Celebrate Diversity:** Embrace the diversity of thoughts, ideas, and backgrounds in your personal and professional life. Encourage open discussions, listen to different perspectives, and create an inclusive environment.

My company celebrates diversity by organizing team-building activities and encouraging the sharing of diverse perspectives during brainstorming sessions. This fosters an environment where everyone feels valued and included, leading to a more harmonious and creative work environment.

7. **Practice Gratitude:** Gratitude can profoundly impact relationships and work environments. By expressing appreciation for the efforts and contributions of others, you create a positive atmosphere that nurtures harmony.

At work, I make it a point to recognize the achievements and efforts of my team members. This boosts their morale and reinforces a culture of appreciation and collaboration.

8. **Lead by Example:** As a leader, your actions significantly impact the harmony of your work environment. Practice what you preach and lead by example. This will inspire your team to follow suit and contribute to a harmonious atmosphere.

In my journey as an entrepreneur, leading with integrity, empathy, and open communication has fostered a harmonious work environment.

In conclusion, cultivating harmony in relationships and work environments requires conscious effort, effective communication, and emotional intelligence. You can create an atmosphere of trust, respect, and cooperation by setting boundaries, resolving conflicts effectively, celebrating diversity, practicing gratitude, and leading by example. This harmonious ecosystem nurtures personal and professional growth and contributes to your overall well-being and success. After all, harmony, like a beautiful symphony, is not a solo performance but the culmination of each note working in synchrony.

As we move into Section 3, we'll delve into inner peace and serenity. Because in this chaotic world, the most precious sanctuary is the one that resides within you. But how do you cultivate that tranquility amidst the storm? Let's embark on this journey to find your inner peace and sanctuary.

The Peaceful Queen: Cultivating Inner Peace and Harmony

The world around us may be in constant flux, but our internal world has the potential to be an oasis of calm and tranquility. Cultivating inner peace is more than a means to an end; it is the pathway to enduring happiness and success. Here are the strategies I have used to foster inner peace and harmony in my own life:

1. **Mindfulness:** Being present in the moment is a powerful tool for cultivating inner peace. Mindfulness helps us disconnect from the external noise and connect with our inner selves. Simple activities like focusing

on your breath or observing the sensations in your body can help you stay grounded in the present. I start each day with a short mindfulness meditation, which helps me focus and maintain a calm demeanor throughout the day.

2. **Self-Compassion:** We often judge ourselves more harshly than we judge others. But self-criticism only adds to our stress and takes away our peace. Instead, try practicing self-compassion. Acknowledge your feelings, accept your flaws, and forgive yourself for your mistakes. This self-compassion has been a critical part of my journey to inner peace.

3. **Emotional Self-Care:** Caring for your emotional health is essential for inner peace. This involves recognizing and expressing your emotions in healthy ways and seeking support when you need it. Whenever I feel overwhelmed, I journal my thoughts and feelings. This helps me gain perspective and manage my emotions effectively.

4. **Physical Health:** Our physical health dramatically impacts our mental and emotional well-being. Regular exercise, a balanced diet, and adequate sleep are crucial for maintaining inner peace. I have made a commitment to prioritize my physical health, which has profoundly impacted my overall sense of peace and well-being.

5. **Positive Affirmations:** The way we talk to ourselves influences our thoughts, emotions, and behaviors. Positive affirmations can help reframe negative thought patterns and foster a positive mindset. I often repeat affirmations like "I am calm and centered" or "I handle challenges with grace and resilience," especially in stressful situations.

6. **Gratitude:** Practicing gratitude shifts our focus from what's wrong to what's right. This shift in perspective can bring about a sense of peace and contentment. I maintain a daily gratitude journal, writing down three things I am grateful for daily.

7. **Letting Go:** Holding onto past hurts, failures, or fears only disturbs our peace. On the other hand, letting go frees us from these negative emotions and allows us to move forward. I have found that forgiveness both of myself and others has been critical in my journey to inner peace.

8. **Connecting with Nature:** Nature has a calming effect on our minds and bodies. Spending time in nature, or even viewing scenes of wilderness, reduces stress and increases feelings of peace and tranquility. I make it a point to spend time outdoors every day, whether walking in the park or for a few minutes in my garden.

In conclusion, cultivating inner peace involves caring for our physical health, practicing mindfulness, self-compassion, emotional self-care, using positive affirmations, practicing gratitude, letting go of past hurts, and connecting with nature. By implementing these strategies daily, we can nurture our inner peace and create a sanctuary within ourselves.

As we move into Section 4, we will tackle the art of adaptability. In the ever-evolving landscape of life, the ability to flex and bend is not just a nice-to-have but a necessity. How can we grow more resilient in the face of change and uncertainty? Let's explore the strategies to help you become a Flexible Queen, adept at navigating life's shifting tides.

The Flexible Queen: Adapting to Changing Priorities and Needs

In entrepreneurship, and indeed in life, change is the only constant. The ability to adapt to shifting circumstances and changing priorities is a crucial determinant of success. In this section, I will share the strategies I have used to cultivate flexibility and adaptability in my own life and career:

1. **Embrace Change:** The first step to adaptability is accepting that change is inevitable. Many of us fear change because it brings uncertainty. However, when

we embrace change, we can turn uncertainty into opportunity. Throughout my entrepreneurial journey, I have learned to view change not as a threat but as an invitation to innovate and grow.

2. **Stay Curious:** Curiosity is a powerful ally in the face of change. It encourages us to seek new information, explore different perspectives, and stay open to new possibilities. By fostering a mindset of curiosity, we can better understand and navigate the changing landscapes around us.

3. **Foster Resilience:** Resilience is the ability to bounce back from adversity or failure. It allows us to keep going in the face of challenges and adapt to new circumstances. I have found that resilience can be cultivated through mindfulness, self-compassion, and maintaining a positive outlook.

4. **Cultivate Emotional Agility:** Emotional agility involves navigating our emotions in a way that serves our best interests. This includes recognizing and validating our feelings and choosing actions that align with our values and goals. By cultivating emotional agility, we can adapt to changing circumstances without getting swept away by our emotions.

5. **Practice Problem-Solving:** Problem-solving skills are crucial for adaptability. They enable us to identify solutions and make decisions in uncertainty. I regular-

ly practice problem-solving by challenging myself to think outside the box and consider multiple solutions to a problem.

6. **Develop a Growth Mindset:** A growth mindset involves viewing challenges as opportunities for learning and growth rather than threats. This mindset fosters adaptability by encouraging us to embrace new experiences, learn from our mistakes, and persist in facing setbacks.

7. **Maintain a Balanced Lifestyle:** A balanced lifestyle supports our physical, emotional, and mental well-being, enabling us to better cope with change and stress. This includes maintaining a healthy diet, regular physical activity, adequate sleep, and engaging in activities that we enjoy and that relax us.

8. **Invest in Continuous Learning:** The world constantly evolves, and staying relevant requires continuous learning. This can involve formal education, self-study, or learning from others. I dedicate time each week to learning something new, whether it's a new skill, concept, or perspective.

9. **Cultivate Strong Relationships:** Strong relationships provide us with support, encouragement, and different perspectives, all of which can help us adapt to change. By nurturing our relationships, we can build a supportive network that will be there for us in times

of change and uncertainty.

10. **Practice Mindfulness:** Mindfulness allows us to stay present and aware, better understand our circumstances, and respond effectively. Whether it's through meditation, mindful movement, or simply taking a few moments each day to tune into our senses, mindfulness can enhance our adaptability.

In conclusion, becoming a Flexible Queen involves embracing change, staying curious, fostering resilience, cultivating emotional agility, practicing problem-solving, developing a growth mindset, maintaining a balanced lifestyle, investing in continuous learning, cultivating strong relationships, and practicing mindfulness. By incorporating these strategies into our lives, we can enhance our ability to adapt to changing circumstances and navigate life's uncertainties with grace and resilience.

As we approach the conclusion of this transformative journey, it's time to reflect on the lessons learned, the strategies discovered, and the personal growth that has been achieved. How can these insights be harnessed to create a thriving business and a fulfilling life, you may ask? Let's consolidate our wisdom and move forward with renewed purpose and clarity.

The Future Belongs to the Balanced

As we stand at the precipice of this incredible journey, looking back at the insights and experiences we've shared, the lessons we've learned, and the wisdom we've accrued, it's time for us to take a moment to reflect. We've known about balance and harmony, the importance of nurturing our relationships, the tranquility of inner peace, and the necessity of adaptability in the ever-changing landscape of life and business. We must integrate these insights into our lives and forge our path forward.

We've learned from the remarkable Queen Nefertiti, whose rule was marked by harmony and balance. From her, we've discovered the power of cultivating a balanced approach to life and its potential for achieving personal and professional success.

We've also drawn inspiration from contemporary leaders like Indra Nooyi, who, during her tenure as CEO of Pepsi-Co, managed to strike a balance between the company's financial success and its impact on society and the environment. We've learned from the resilience and adaptability of women like Mary Barra, the first female CEO of a major global automaker, General Motors. She led the company through a significant crisis and emerged stronger and more resilient, showing us the importance of adaptability and perseverance in adversity.

Let's also acknowledge the power of inner peace, beautifully exemplified by the life of Mother Teresa, who found serenity amidst chaos and dedicated her life to serving the poor and the needy. Her life teaches us peace starts from within and extends outward, influencing our relationships, work, and world.

As we step into the future, it's crucial to remember the four fundamental principles we've discussed:

1. **Balance:** Make conscious decisions to balance your work and personal life. Create a schedule that accommodates your professional commitments and personal needs. Avoid overworking and remember to take time for self-care and relaxation.

2. **Harmony:** Strive to build harmonious relationships in your personal and professional life. Learn to communicate effectively, understand the needs of others, and work towards creating a positive and supportive environment.

3. **Inner Peace:** Develop practices that promote inner peace, such as meditation, mindfulness, or yoga. Learn to manage stress effectively and nurture a positive mindset.

4. **Adaptability:** Be ready to adapt to changes in your life and business. Embrace challenges as opportunities

for growth and learning.

Let's transform these principles into actionable steps:

Action Steps:

1. **Create a Balanced Schedule:** Set clear boundaries between work and personal life. Allocate specific times for work, relaxation, and individual activities.

2. **Cultivate Harmonious Relationships:** Invest time and effort into nurturing your relationships. Practice active listening and empathy, and be supportive of others.

3. **Practice Inner Peace:** Incorporate mindfulness practices into your daily routine. Spend a few minutes each day in quiet reflection or meditation.

4. **Embrace Adaptability:** Be open to change and adjust your plans as needed. View challenges as opportunities for growth.

And finally, as we conclude this chapter, let's draw upon the wisdom of another incredible woman, the American astronaut Mae Jemison, who once said,

"Never limit yourself because of others' limited imagination; never limit others because of your own limited imagination."

This mantra serves as a reminder of the limitless potential within each of us. It urges us to break free from the constraints of societal expectations and to create our own path.

Remember, the future belongs to the balance. Embrace the journey and step into the realm of infinite possibilities.

Chapter Twelve

THE REIGN OF A QUEEN

The Queen's Journey Begins

G ROWING UP, I WAS always enamored with the stories of legendary women leaders. Their courage, resilience, and unwavering commitment to their visions were sources of endless inspiration for me. In this regard, no one was quite as captivating as Queen Nefertiti. Here was a woman who not only led but did so with such grace, strength, and innovation that she left an indelible mark on history.

My own journey as an entrepreneur was challenging. Like many women starting out in business, I faced numerous obstacles, from societal biases to internal doubts about my abilities. I found myself constantly comparing my progress to my peers, and the weight of these comparisons became a heavy burden. It was a battle that felt uphill, yet I was determined to create my empire.

The breakthrough came during a trip to Egypt, where I got the opportunity to learn about the legacy of Queen Nefertiti. Walking through the ancient ruins, I was captivated by the stories of her reign. Her fearless approach to leadership, her unyielding commitment to her people, and her relentless pursuit of innovation were characteristics I deeply admired. It was a revelation that led me to reassess my own approach to leadership and entrepreneurship.

The more I learned about Nefertiti, the more I realized that my journey echoed hers in many ways. Like her, I was navigating uncharted territories, faced with the daunting task of leading and making a difference. And like her, I was driven by a vision of creating something bigger than myself.

Nefertiti was a woman of strength, grace, and intelligence who ruled at a time when female leaders were rare. She was known to have played a significant role in a religious revolution, ushering in the worship of one god, Aten, and moving the royal court to a new city, Akhenaten. Despite resistance, she stood firm in her convictions, showing a remarkable blend of empathy, resilience, and strategic acumen.

Emulating Nefertiti's leadership approach, I began to transform my own. I took calculated risks, aligned my actions with my core values, and, most importantly, cultivated resilience. Over time, I noticed a change in my business and myself. I was becoming more confident, more decisive, and more innovative. I was evolving into the leader I aspired to be, all while expanding my empire.

Today's world is much different from Nefertiti's, yet the struggles faced by women leaders have threads of similarity. A powerful example is Angela Merkel, Germany's first female Chancellor, 's remarkable leadership journey. Despite being in a male-dominated political sphere, Merkel's leadership, characterized by her pragmatic approach and unyielding resilience, made her one of the most influential leaders in the world.

For us, as women entrepreneurs, there are valuable lessons to be learned from these women. This chapter promises to delve deeper into their journeys and explore the traits that made them unstoppable. These are traits that every woman entrepreneur can harness to not only expand her empire but do so with grace, resilience, and unwavering dedication.

In the upcoming sections, we will explore the qualities of a regal, empathetic, visionary, and unstoppable queen. Each section is designed to draw from the experiences of these women, guiding you toward becoming an unstoppable force in your own right.

Section 1 will uncover the secrets behind embodying the qualities of a powerful and regal leader. Section 2 will delve into the importance of practicing empathy and compassion towards others. Section 3 will teach us how to be a visionary, continuously innovating and expanding our empire. Finally, in Section 4, we will draw lessons from these remarkable women about creating a legacy of success and empowerment as unstoppable woman entrepreneurs.

To conclude this journey, I want to emphasize a common thread in the stories of Queen Nefertiti and Angela Merkel. They both had a profound understanding of their capabilities and a clear vision for their realms. But what made them truly remarkable was their ability to rise above societal norms and create lasting change. This change was not just in their respective domains but in the hearts and minds of those they led.

My journey has been a testament to the transformative power of embracing leadership qualities inspired by these women. There were moments of doubt and fear, but my resolve never wavered. And in the end, I emerged stronger, wiser, and more determined.

As we navigate the following sections, I invite you to reflect on your journey. Consider the obstacles you've faced and the victories you've claimed. These experiences are your stepping stones to becoming a queen in your own right.

And remember, no matter the scale of your empire or the challenges you face, you have the strength and the capacity to overcome. Just as Nefertiti did in ancient Egypt and Merkel in modern Germany. Just as I did in the world of entrepreneurship. And just as you will in your journey.

Your reign is about to unfold. Are you ready to embrace it?

Now, let us delve into the first section, where we will uncover the secrets behind embodying the qualities of a powerful and regal leader.

The Regal Queen - Embodying the Qualities of a Powerful Leader

When I was just beginning my entrepreneurial journey, I remember looking up to several successful business leaders and entrepreneurs. Their decisiveness, vision, and resilience inspired me. However, the more I delved into their leadership styles, the more I realized something profound: they were not born leaders. Leadership, like any other skill, is developed over time. They had to cultivate and embody specific qualities that eventually crowned them as regal leaders of their domains.

A pivotal point in my entrepreneurial journey came when I had to make a difficult decision that would potentially alter the course of my business. I had an opportunity to expand my business into a new market, but it required significant investment and risk. I spent countless hours deliberating, consulting with advisors, and weighing the pros and cons. The fear of failure was palpable, yet I knew the enormous growth potential. At that moment, I realized that being a regal leader meant being decisive and courageous, even when the stakes were high. So, I took the leap of faith, which paid off in ways I had never imagined. Today, that decision remains one of the significant turning points in my business journey.

To further illustrate this, let's delve into the life of Queen Nefertiti of Egypt, one of the most influential queens of ancient times. Nefertiti, whose name means "the beautiful one has come," was not just known for her extraordinary beauty but for her strategic vision and leadership.

Nefertiti ruled alongside her husband, Pharaoh Akhenaten, in the 14th century B.C. During her reign, she played a crucial role in religious reforms that shifted Egypt from polytheism to monotheism, worshiping one sun god, Aten. This highly controversial move challenged the established religious order, putting Nefertiti at the center of public scrutiny and potential rebellion.

Despite the mounting pressure and threats to her rule, Nefertiti stood firm in her decision. She understood the long-term vision behind their religious reform - a unified

Egypt under one god. Her ability to stand by her conviction, despite the controversy and pushback, truly encapsulates the courage and determination characteristic of a regal queen.

This pivotal moment in Nefertiti's reign taught me that to be a regal queen in my domain, I needed to be more than just an entrepreneur. I had to be a visionary with the courage to pursue my convictions, no matter how unorthodox they might seem.

As we move forward, remember that embodying the qualities of a regal queen doesn't require a royal bloodline or a golden crown. Instead, it requires developing and nurturing leadership qualities that empower you to make decisive choices, take calculated risks, and stay true to your vision.

In the next section, we will explore how to practice empathy and compassion towards others, another crucial aspect of a regal queen's leadership. Are you ready to continue your journey into regal leadership?

Continuing our exploration of regal leadership, I was once faced with a situation that required a compassionate approach. My company was in the throes of a significant setback. We had lost a major client, and morale was low. As a leader, I was torn between putting on a brave face and hiding my disappointment or showing my team my vulnerability. After much thought, I chose the latter. I had an open conversation with my team, sharing my disappointment and encouraging them to voice their feelings.

This approach, although unconventional, turned out to be a game-changer. The level of connection within the team deepened. We rallied together, working on our shortcomings and exploring new opportunities. We emerged from this setback stronger and more united than ever. This experience taught me that being a regal queen does not mean hiding one's emotions. Instead, it involves leading with empathy and compassion, allowing yourself to be human, and connecting with your team on a deeper level.

Nefertiti, too, exemplified this compassionate approach to leadership. Known for her love for her people, she is often depicted in ancient carvings, offering gifts to the needy and providing for her subjects. Despite her lofty status, she did not distance herself from her people's daily struggles and needs. She ruled with a compassionate heart, leaving a lasting legacy that survived centuries.

We can take a page from Nefertiti's book as we navigate our leadership journeys. Empathy and compassion should be at the heart of our interactions and decisions. Whether you're dealing with a team member, a client, or a business partner, approaching each situation with understanding and kindness can create a profound impact.

In summary, embodying the qualities of a regal queen involves leading with courage and conviction, just like I did when I decided to expand my business and like Nefertiti did during her controversial religious reform. It also involves leading with empathy and compassion, creating deep connections with those you lead. We can create a legacy of successful and empowering leadership by adopting these qualities.

In the next section, we will delve into the role of the visionary queen, continuously innovating and expanding her empire. It's about embracing change, spotting opportunities, and driving forward with a clear, compelling vision. Are you ready to continue this journey towards regal leadership? The legacy of the visionary queen awaits.

Entrepreneurship is ever-changing, but the true visionary queen stands tall amidst the fluctuations. She weathers the storm with an unwavering gaze towards the horizon. Let's venture into the world of Queen Nefertiti and my journey to learn how a visionary queen navigates the complexities of expanding her empire.

The Visionary Queen: Continuously Innovating and Expanding your Empire

Just as Queen Nefertiti dared to dream of a new and revolutionary Egypt, we as women entrepreneurs must dare to envision our businesses in ways previously unimaginable. Predicting the future while keeping a firm grip on the present is a delicate balance. A balance that can be the difference between stagnation and growth, irrelevance, and innovation.

Nefertiti lived in an era of change, where her husband Akhenaten sought to transform ancient Egypt's religious landscape. They dared to dream, to envision a future divergent from the past. This audacity to innovate to challenge the status quo is a characteristic all visionary leaders share.

I recall a time in my entrepreneurial journey when I was at a crossroads. My business had grown beyond my expectations, but it was teetering on the edge of plateauing. The market was evolving, customer needs were changing, and competition was fierce. I knew that to continue growing, I would have to innovate.

Taking inspiration from Nefertiti, I started envisioning my business' future. I visualized how it could adapt to changing market conditions, how it could meet emerging customer needs, and how it could stand out amidst growing competition. I dreamed, just as Nefertiti did, of a future divergent from the present.

This vision guided me toward the path of innovation. I began integrating technology into my operations, providing online services, and embracing sustainable practices. My business evolved, and with it, I developed as a leader.

Yet, envisioning a future and implementing it are two different challenges. One requires imagination; the other involves action. A visionary queen knows that a dream without action is merely a hallucination.

So, I embarked on the journey to transform my vision into reality. It was a challenging journey filled with obstacles and setbacks. But my vision, my dream of an innovative and successful business, propelled me forward.

And the result? My business flourished, growing in ways I had only dreamed of. It became a powerhouse in the industry, setting trends rather than following them. All because I dared to be a visionary queen, just like Nefertiti.

Now, let's explore the practical steps to becoming a visionary queen in your own realm:

1. **Imagine the Future:** Begin by visualizing your business' future. Where do you see it in five years? Ten years? How can it evolve to meet changing market conditions and customer needs?

2. **Formulate a Strategy:** Once you have a vision, plan to make it a reality. Identify the steps you need to take,

the resources you need to acquire, and the challenges you must overcome.

3. **Implement Your Plan:** With a plan in place, it's time to take action. Remember, a vision without action is merely a hallucination. Start implementing your plan step by step.

4. **Adapt and Learn:** You will encounter obstacles and setbacks as you implement your plan. Embrace them as learning opportunities. Adapt your plan as necessary and keep moving forward.

5. **Celebrate Success:** Lastly, celebrate your achievements. Every step you take towards your vision, no matter how small, is a success.

Embrace the spirit of Queen Nefertiti, dare to dream, and become the visionary queen of your entrepreneurial empire. The world is waiting for your innovation.

In conclusion, the power of vision must be considered. Queen Nefertiti's reign marked a transformative period in ancient Egypt precisely because she and her husband dared to envision a different future. As a modern-day entrepreneur, you, too, can bring about significant changes in your industry and make your mark. Your vision can guide your enterprise, influence your team, and shape your legacy. Be bold, be courageous, and dare to dream.

Challenges and failures can push us toward success just as the wind propels a ship's sails. The key lies in our attitude: Do we let setbacks stop us, or do we let them drive us forward, strengthening us for the journey ahead? Let's delve into this in the next section.

The Unstoppable Queen: Creating a Legacy of Success and Empowerment as an Unstoppable Woman Entrepreneur

The force of resilience is a defining trait of the unstoppable woman entrepreneur. In business, the journey to success is rarely linear; it often entails stumbling blocks, detours, and outright roadblocks. However, the one who remains undeterred despite these obstacles and adapts to the changing terrain possesses the tenacity of an unstoppable queen.

I recall the period of my early entrepreneurial journey when a significant investment deal fell through. It seemed as if my dreams were crumbling around me, threatening to bury my ambition under a mound of disappointment and self-doubt. Yet, amid the darkness, I remembered Queen Nefertiti's reign, a beacon that guided me back towards resilience and determination.

Nefertiti, faced with significant resistance to her and her husband's monotheistic revolution, demonstrated courage and fortitude in the face of adversity. Many would have cowed to the immense societal and political pressure, but Nefertiti held steadfast to her convictions, embodying the archetype of the unstoppable queen. Her reign is remembered as a time of prosperity and growth, primarily due to her strength and perseverance.

Inspired by Nefertiti's tenacity, I doubled down on my vision and strived even harder to secure the resources needed to propel my venture. As an entrepreneur, the determination to stay the course, adapt, and not be deterred by setbacks can pave the way to success. We may stumble, but it's our decision whether we use that fall as a step toward our ascent.

Adopting this unstoppable mindset necessitates you to value resilience over comfort, progress over perfection, and transformation over stagnation. It is the belief that every failure is not a dead-end but an opportunity to learn, grow, and emerge stronger. Unstoppable entrepreneurs understand that the pathway to success is laid brick by brick, with each setback serving as a stepping stone rather than a stumbling block.

Germany's first female Chancellor, Angela Merkel, embodied this unstoppable attitude throughout her political career. Amidst the Eurozone crisis, she made difficult decisions that drew severe criticism from her political adversaries and allies. Nevertheless, she persisted in her vision for a united and robust European Union, earning her the moniker "The Indestructible." She stayed resilient and guided her nation through a tumultuous period, showcasing the hallmark of an unstoppable leader.

To adopt this unstoppable mindset, start by viewing every challenge as an opportunity for growth. Each setback you encounter in your business is a chance for you to learn, adapt, and emerge stronger.

Next, develop a proactive approach towards failure. Rather than avoiding loss, accept it as an inevitable part of your entrepreneurial journey. Embrace it as a teacher who imparts invaluable lessons for future success.

Then, foster resilience by maintaining a positive mindset. Cultivate an attitude of gratitude and focus on the positive aspects of your life and business. This attitude helps you to navigate the rough waters of entrepreneurship with grace and determination.

Lastly, surround yourself with people who inspire you to become unstoppable. By surrounding yourself with other resilient entrepreneurs, you tap into a well of collective wisdom, gain inspiration, and foster mutual support, aiding your journey to becoming an unstoppable woman entrepreneur.

To conclude, adopting the persona of an unstoppable queen is more than merely being persistent. It's about being resilient, embracing failures as opportunities for learning, maintaining a positive mindset, and surrounding yourself with a supportive community. Like Queen Nefertiti's, your legacy can inspire future generations of women entrepreneurs, encouraging them to be just as resilient and unstoppable.

From shaping an empire in the sands of ancient Egypt to building successful modern businesses, the journey of leadership is an intricate dance of strategy and intuition.

As we move into Section 4, let's dive into how an Unstoppable Queen remains visionary, continuously innovating and expanding her empire, inspired by the wisdom of the ages and guided by a vision of the future. Join me as we uncover the secrets of the visionary queen, turning dreams into reality, one step at a time.

The Visionary Queen: Continuously Innovating and Expanding Your Empire

Just as Nefertiti's reign was marked by a significant cultural revolution, your business empire must evolve with time. Being visionary means breaking the barriers of the conventional, pushing boundaries, and creating new paradigms. It's a perpetual learning journey, exploring uncharted territories and challenging the status quo.

I still remember the day I first incorporated these principles into my business. Faced with a stagnating growth rate, I knew something had to change. Looking back, I see that the transformation of my enterprise took time. I had to constantly question the existing business model, innovate, and adopt a future-focused mindset.

The first step is cultivating a growth mindset. A visionary leader sees failures not as stumbling blocks but as stepping stones towards success. When a particular strategy did not bring the expected results in my business, I analyzed the situation, learned from it, and formulated a better plan instead of letting it be a deterrent.

Secondly, empower your team. Nefertiti's reign was characterized by her trust in her advisors and artisans, empowering them to create the revolutionary art that defined her era. Similarly, I found success in entrusting my team with more responsibilities. I encouraged them to bring new ideas to the table, fostering a culture of innovation.

Thirdly, embrace technology. The business world today is inextricably linked with technology. Like Angela Merkel, who played a crucial role in Germany's digital transformation, adopting the latest tech advancements and integrating them into your business operations can drive your business growth exponentially.

Lastly, keep your finger on the pulse of your industry. Being visionary also means anticipating changes and being prepared for them. I regularly participated in industry conferences, stayed abreast with the latest news, and watched trends closely. It enabled me to foresee market changes and adapt my business strategies accordingly.

A visionary leader is also a risk-taker. When I decided to venture into a new market segment, it was a significant risk. But as the saying goes, "No risk, no reward." It was a game-changer for my business, increasing customer base and revenue.

In her time, Nefertiti would not have been revered as a visionary leader if she had not dared to defy the norms and dream the impossible. Her audacity to envision a society worshipping a single deity, the sun disc Aten, demonstrated her visionary prowess. It left an indelible impact, turning her reign into an era of unparalleled prosperity and artistic splendor.

Let the reign of Nefertiti inspire you to become a visionary queen of your empire. Keep innovating, keep dreaming, and keep expanding. The horizon is far, but it's within your reach.

To wrap up this section, the action steps are:

1. Cultivate a growth mindset and learn from failures.

2. Empower your team and foster a culture of innovation.

3. Embrace technology to streamline operations and improve productivity.

4. Stay updated with industry trends and anticipate changes.

5. Be a risk-taker and venture into new market segments.

That concludes Section 4 of our journey. As we end, remember that your empire awaits your visionary prowess. In the next section, we will explore how to become an unstoppable queen who creates a legacy of success and empowerment.

We have journeyed through the power of a queen's reign, delved into the depths of compassion and empathy, and traversed the realm of innovation and expansion. We're about to culminate our expedition, tying together all these vibrant threads into a strong fabric of success and empowerment. So, brace yourself for the final stretch, where we distill the essence of a genuinely Unstoppable Queen.

The Unstoppable Queen: Conclusion

And so, we draw the curtains on the illustrious reign of a Queen, an adventure woven through the hearts of leaders past and present. From Nefertiti's time-honored rule to contemporary icons of leadership like Oprah Winfrey, Sara Blakely, Melinda Gates, and Arianna Huffington, we have voyaged through the qualities of Queens, extraordinary women who have forever imprinted their names in the annals of history.

As we moved from the regal presence of a Queen to the empathetic heartbeat that pulses within her, we began to understand that the essence of Queenship is not merely about commanding respect or exhibiting power. No, it is about a profound understanding of the human condition, a compassionate resonance connecting her with her subjects' aspirations and challenges. I've experienced this firsthand in my mentorship journey with a young entrepreneur. The shared struggles, the shared victories they reminded me that authentic leadership stems from empathetic engagement.

Visionary leadership was our next sojourn, a realm where a Queen not only dreams but molds her dreams into reality. Queen Nefertiti expanded her empire, pushing the boundaries of what was known, and today, women leaders like Melinda Gates echo this pioneering spirit, transforming lives through the power of technology. My own experiences underscored this journey, proving that vision is only as grand if we are willing to take bold strides toward it.

And then, we encountered the spirit of an unstoppable Queen. A spirit that cannot be subdued by setbacks, a resilient spirit, a spirit that is relentless in its pursuit of creating an indelible legacy. Queens like Oprah Winfrey and Sara Blakely personify this resilience, their success stories a testament to the power of determination and unwavering resolve. Their stories mirrored my own, reinforcing the belief that to be an unstoppable Queen, one must rise from the ashes of failure, stronger and more determined.

So, what promise awaits you at the end of this journey? It is the promise of transformation, of metamorphosing into an Unstoppable Queen who carries herself with dignity, leads with compassion, dreams with audacity, and whose spirit is unyielding in the face of adversities. This journey beckons you to don the mantle of Queenship and inspire a change in your world.

Before we bid adieu, allow me to leave you with five detailed action steps that will guide you in your continuing journey as a Queen:

1. **Reflect on Your Leadership:** Spend some quiet moments every day, looking at your reflection and recognizing your strengths and potential. The queen

you see in the mirror today is a leader, but she is also a student, forever willing to learn and grow. Take inspiration from women like Arianna Huffington, who underlines the importance of reflection and introspection for personal growth.

2. **Cultivate Empathy:** Make a conscious effort to understand the needs, dreams, and aspirations of those around you. This means active listening, open communication, and genuine interest in others' welfare. Remember, Melinda Gates started her philanthropy journey by understanding the lives she wanted to impact.

3. **Be a Visionary:** Challenge yourself to think beyond the confines of the now. Allow yourself to dream big, and don't shy away from setting ambitious goals. Take it from Sara Blakely, who turned a simple idea into a billion-dollar business nothing is impossible for a visionary.

4. **Embrace Resilience:** Recognize that setbacks are a part of your journey. When you stumble, find the strength to rise. Let the stories of Oprah Winfrey, who overcame countless hurdles, inspire you to see setbacks as stepping stones to success.

5. **Build Your Legacy:** Begin with the end in mind. Ask yourself, "What legacy do I want to leave behind?" Every decision you make and every step you take

should be a stride towards building that legacy. Just as Nefertiti has her place in history, should you aim to make a difference that will be remembered?

These steps may not transform you into a Queen overnight, but they will guide you on a path that leads to Queenship, a journey that is as transformative as it is enriching. As you navigate this journey, remember to celebrate every victory, no matter how small, and learn from every setback, no matter how daunting.

Finally, as we conclude this chapter, I want to leave you with a mantra, a guiding beacon as you journey towards becoming the Unstoppable Queen. Let these words echo in your heart, invigorate your spirit, and steer your path:

"I am a Queen. I lead with grace, love with compassion, dream with courage, and rise with resilience."

These words aren't mere affirmations. They are a testament to the extraordinary power that lies within you. They are a promise of the remarkable journey that awaits you. They are a tribute to the indomitable spirit of Queenship that you are destined to embody.

We began our journey together, traversing through the reigns of legendary Queens, meandering through personal stories, and diving into lessons of leadership and resilience. Now, it's your turn to carve your own path, lead with your heart, dream with audacity, and rise with strength. You are ready. You are an Unstoppable Queen.

As we wrap up this chapter, remember that the journey of a Queen is not easy, but it brings immense joy and fulfillment. You have been given the tools and insights to chart your own course and rule your kingdom. So, rise, Unstoppable Queen. Your reign awaits.

THE UNSTOPPABLE JOURNEY

IN THE QUIET HOURS of the early morning, the world still blanketed in the velvet touch of night, I sat at my desk. The house was quiet, except for the gentle hum of the computer and the sporadic keys tapping beneath my fingers. In these moments of solitude and silence, I found a reflective stillness, a chance to look back at the journey that brought me here.

I remember when I was just a young woman, stepping out into the world for the first time an ocean of dreams in my heart and a constellation of ideas whirling in my head. I had always wanted to create something of my own, to carve my path and leave a mark on this world. Entrepreneurship was not just a choice for me; it was a calling.

Like me, Queen Nefertiti, the esteemed pharaoh of Ancient Egypt, began her journey as an unknown woman with a promise of greatness. From the shards of history and time, we know her as a woman of remarkable beauty and intellect, an influential figure who etched her legacy in the annals of time. Despite the millenniums that separate us, I feel a strange camaraderie with the queen, a shared experience of holding power and influence in our hands and using it to shape our destinies.

Nefertiti's reign was marked by a transformational era in Egyptian history. She and her husband, Pharaoh Akhenaten, uprooted the traditional polytheistic religion and replaced it with a monotheistic one. They built a whole new city, Akhenaten, where they ruled from. The queen, known for her strong character and influential role, was not just a figurehead. She actively participated in these changes, standing as a driving force in the religious revolution.

In my own journey, I saw reflections of Nefertiti's strength and resilience. I, too, faced a time of radical change when I took the plunge and started my business. It was a time of uncertainty, sleepless nights, and endless worries. Yet, like Nefertiti, I chose to embrace the challenge, face the odds, and transform not just my life but the lives of those around me.

My journey was filled with twists and turns, victories and setbacks, joy and despair. Sometimes, I doubted myself, questioned my decisions, and feared for the future. Yet, I learned, grew, and emerged stronger with each stumble and fall.

In the same way, Nefertiti faced her share of trials and tribulations. Her monotheistic revolution was met with resistance. Yet, she stood firm, unyielding, her vision of a new world order unclouded by the tumult around her.

Her story reminds me that to be a woman, a leader, and an entrepreneur is to embrace change and the inherent challenges that come with it. It is about being brave enough to take the road less traveled, to forge a path where none existed.

This journey we embarked on, Nefertiti and I, thousands of years apart, is not just ours. It's a journey shared by countless women who dared to dream, defy, create, and lead. It's a journey of transformation and growth, breaking barriers and shattering glass ceilings.

The promise for you, dear reader, is that you, too, can embark on this journey. It's a journey not just of building a successful business but also of self-discovery, of finding your strength and your voice. As we delve into this journey, we will explore the strategies and techniques to create a sustainable, independent business that thrives without your constant oversight. We will delve into leadership, learning to steer your ship and navigate the turbulent seas of entrepreneurship. And most importantly, we will learn to embrace the journey with all its highs and lows, savoring the lessons along the way.

There are four crucial aspects we will uncover:

First, we will delve into the importance of embracing change and adaptation, learning from Nefertiti's religious revolution and how it influenced the kingdom. In the same way, being open to change and adaptable can significantly impact your business and its growth.

Second, we will explore the value of resilience and unwavering determination in adversity, drawing inspiration from my journey and the countless hurdles I faced and overcame. This tenacity allows us to weather the storms and emerge stronger.

Third, we will delve into the power of transformational leadership. Just as Nefertiti stood beside Akhenaten, leading the radical changes, we too can transform our businesses by leading from the front, inspiring and driving our teams towards a shared vision.

Lastly, we will emphasize the importance of leaving a legacy, of building something that outlives us, much like Nefertiti's legacy that lives on centuries after her reign.

Embracing Change and Adaptation

In every entrepreneur's journey, there comes a point when change is inevitable. Much like Nefertiti's time, the business world is constantly in flux, with innovations disrupting industries overnight. As women entrepreneurs, our ability to adapt to these changes can be the deciding factor between growth and stagnation.

I recall a time in the early years of my entrepreneurship journey when my business was at a crossroads. The online retail industry, where my business was deeply rooted, was undergoing massive technological changes. The advent of new e-commerce platforms and the shift in consumer behavior towards online shopping were upending traditional retail models.

Instead of resisting the change, I chose to embrace it. But it was a challenging decision. The fear of unknown territory was confirmed, the challenges seemed insurmountable, and the road ahead was unclear. I felt like I was standing on the edge of a precipice, contemplating whether to leap into the unknown.

Just as Nefertiti and Akhenaten made the audacious decision to shift Egypt's religious belief system, I, too, made a bold move. I decided to pivot my business model from traditional retail to e-commerce, transforming my entire business structure.

The transition could have been smoother. There were technical challenges, resistance from team members, and even a dip in sales as we struggled to establish our brand in a new marketplace. But we persisted, learning, adapting, and improving along the way.

Much like Nefertiti's reign, which ushered in an era of prosperity and artistic freedom, the transformation of my business brought about unprecedented growth and opportunities. We were able to reach a global market, expand our product offerings, and, most importantly, serve our customers better.

Nefertiti's radical change still echoes today, visible in her popularized Amarna art style, which marked a significant departure from traditional Egyptian art. Similarly, the shift in my business approach has left a lasting impact. It has created a culture of adaptability within my team, where we continually seek to innovate and improve.

The lesson here, dear reader, is that as women entrepreneurs, we must view change not as a threat but as an opportunity for growth and innovation. The business world is evolving rapidly, and we must grow with it. We need to be bold, fearless, and ready to disrupt the status quo like Nefertiti.

As you tread your entrepreneurial journey, remember this: change is not the enemy; stagnation is. Adaptability is not an option; it's a survival tool. The more willing you are to adjust and evolve, the more resilient your business will be against the tides of change.

Section 2 will delve into the power of vision and determination. Just as Nefertiti held fast to her revolutionary vision for Egypt despite opposition, we, as women entrepreneurs, must persevere in the face of adversity. Remember, our dreams are not quickly shattered; they are not fragile but resilient, awaiting the right moment to blossom. Prepare to explore unwavering commitment and unwaning courage, the authentic armor of any successful entrepreneur. Are you ready to dive into Section 2?

Vision and Determination

Who would it be if I asked you to name an entrepreneur whose vision and determination had impacted you? Is it a famous figure, someone closer to home, a friend, a family member, or even yourself? There is no one better to exemplify these qualities than Queen Nefertiti. Nefertiti, which translates to "the beautiful one has come," stood out as a beacon of change during her reign in ancient Egypt. She and her husband Akhenaten envisioned an Egypt that broke the traditional boundaries of religion, promoting the worship of one god - Aten, the sun disk.

This vision was steeped in controversy and opposed by the established priesthood, which had long been used to polytheism. Yet, Nefertiti was not deterred. She recognized the transformative power of her vision and how it could change Egypt's social and religious landscape. Similarly, as women entrepreneurs, we, too, must see the transformative power within our visions. In doing so, we align ourselves with the courage and resilience to turn our dreams into reality.

My journey as an entrepreneur began with a vision to empower women in the business landscape. As a woman in the world of entrepreneurship, I saw first-hand the challenges and barriers we faced. These ranged from societal stereotypes and gender inequality to a lack of access to resources. I knew something needed to change. Much like Nefertiti, I chose to go against the current, swimming upstream with the firm belief that my vision could change the status quo.

In the early days of my entrepreneurial journey, the odds were stacked against me. Doubts crept in, and voices whispered that I was fighting a losing battle, but I held onto my vision. I reminded myself daily of its transformative power, the lives it could change, and the ripple effect it could create in the world. The process was grueling, but it was in this crucible of trials that my determination was fortified.

Like Queen Nefertiti, there were moments of backlash, moments when others questioned the feasibility of my vision. But determination, fueled by a powerful vision, can surmount difficulties. I was resolute, persistent, and unwavering in my commitment to my entrepreneurial journey. I knew that my dream of creating a platform for women in business wasn't just about me-it was a collective dream shared by many.

Much like Nefertiti's innovative religious reforms left a lasting impression on ancient Egypt, my relentless efforts eventually bore fruit. Women began to engage with the platforms and resources I had created. Success stories began to emerge, each validating the power of the vision that had been the compass guiding my journey.

Every victory, every setback, every late night, every "no" that eventually turned into a "yes" helped shape the woman I am today-an unstoppable entrepreneur. I share this story to illustrate the transformative power of vision and determination. Nefertiti's determination to realize her vision despite opposition was the foundation for her impactful reign, a lesson I carried with me throughout my journey.

As we navigate our entrepreneurial journeys, let's cultivate an unwavering vision and determination to match. Both are essential ingredients to success. As you continue to face challenges and obstacles in your path, remember the story of Nefertiti. Consider her unwavering determination and the lasting impact she made in her world. Just as she did, you, too, hold the power to change the landscape of your field through your vision and determination.

Now, it's time to turn this reflection into actionable steps. Is your vision clearly defined? How are you nurturing your determination? As we move forward into the next section, we will explore ways to promote and harness these two powerful forces to bring about change in our respective fields.

As we embark on the final stages of our journey, it is crucial to remember the importance of resilience and transformation. As entrepreneurial women, how can we cultivate these qualities to build an empire that stands the test of time? Let's delve deeper into this exciting challenge.

Cultivating Resilience and Transformation

Every entrepreneurial journey is a thrilling adventure filled with unexpected twists and turns. As we traverse through this unpredictable terrain, our resilience is constantly put to the test. This was a lesson I learned early in my career.

The setback I faced in the early days of my entrepreneurial journey was an experience that, at the time, felt like a severe blow. After putting all my effort into a project, the client unexpectedly pulled out just as we were about to launch. I was devastated. It felt like all my hard work and investment had been for nothing.

But as I dusted myself off, I saw the situation differently. Yes, I had experienced a setback. But it wasn't the end of my journey. I was not a failure. It was simply a hiccup, a pause, an opportunity to reassess and build an even stronger foundation.

And that's precisely what I did. I examined what had gone wrong, learned from my mistakes, and then got back on my feet. With new insights and a more robust plan, I moved forward. This experience taught me a crucial lesson about the importance of resilience in entrepreneurship.

Resilience is more than just bouncing back from failure. It's about developing the mental and emotional fortitude to navigate obstacles and keep pushing forward, even when the odds are against you. It's about learning from your mistakes and turning them into stepping stones for success.

And just as the phoenix rises from its ashes, our businesses can emerge stronger from their setbacks. The key lies in our ability to transform. Transformation is not about becoming something entirely new. Instead, it's about evolving, adapting, and improving based on our experiences and the changing landscape.

As entrepreneurs, we must constantly transform to meet market trends and customer needs. This might mean revising our business strategies, embracing new technologies, or diversifying our product or service offerings. Like Queen Nefertiti, who left a lasting legacy through her transformative leadership, we, too, can make a significant impact through our ability to adapt and evolve.

Transformation goes hand in hand with resilience. While resilience helps us navigate challenges and setbacks, transformation allows us to leverage these experiences to innovate and grow our businesses.

So, how can we cultivate resilience and transformation in our entrepreneurial journey? How can we use these qualities to build a sustainable, impactful, and rewarding empire? The following section will explore practical strategies to do just that.

As we delve into the final part of our reflection, we'll delve deeper into understanding the true essence of our resilience and transformative capacities. We'll examine how they function as twin pillars of a successful entrepreneurial journey and discover practical strategies for fostering these crucial qualities. Ready for the final leap? Let's explore these empowering pathways to our royal ascension, just as Queen Nefertiti did in her time.

Implementing Transformation Strategies

Queen Nefertiti's transformative journey was not just a product of fate but the result of her conscious choices and efforts. Her resilience and adaptability were her most reliable weapons as she navigated through the turbulent currents of ancient politics. As the queen of Egypt, she continuously adapted her strategies to ensure her vision for a prosperous and harmonious kingdom became a reality. She did not flinch when met with challenges but viewed them as opportunities to learn, grow, and refine her strategies.

Akin to her, every entrepreneurial journey requires such a transformative mindset. It calls for a readiness to adapt and innovate, navigate uncertainties, and transform challenges into opportunities. Let's explore effective strategies to foster these qualities in our entrepreneurial endeavors.

1. Embracing Uncertainty and Change:

In a world of constant change, success belongs to those who adapt quickly and effectively. But change often carries a sense of uncertainty, and it is natural for us to feel apprehensive. However, remember that the same uncertainty also bears potential for new possibilities.

One of my clients, Sarah, was a successful executive in a technology firm. When a sudden market shift threatened her company's relevance, she didn't panic. Instead, she chose to view it as an opportunity to innovate. Her team began exploring new technological trends and investing in research and development. Today, her company is a pioneering player in a novel tech arena, all thanks to her willingness to embrace change and uncertainty.

2. Cultivating Emotional Intelligence:

Entrepreneurship is not just about business acumen; it involves significant emotional intelligence. Understanding and managing our emotions can help us make better decisions, deal with stress, and interact effectively with team members and clients.

In my own experience, developing emotional intelligence was a game-changer. Earlier in my career, I often felt overwhelmed by the stresses associated with entrepreneurship. It began to take a toll on my health and relationships. However, as I started practicing mindfulness and emotional regulation, I noticed a significant improvement in my stress management and overall productivity.

3. Building a Learning Culture:

Queen Nefertiti wasn't born with all the wisdom she exhibited. She, too, was a learner. As entrepreneurs, we must foster a learning culture within our organizations and ourselves. Encourage your team members to upskill, provide them with learning opportunities, and lead by example. A culture of learning breeds innovation and adaptability.

One of my clients, a startup founder, prioritizes learning within his organization. He sets aside a budget for employee education and encourages knowledge-sharing sessions. As a result, his team is continually innovating and adapting to changes, making his startup a formidable player in its industry.

4. Developing a Resilient Mindset:

The entrepreneurial journey is a marathon, not a sprint. It requires a resilient mindset to keep going despite challenges and failures. Resilience is about viewing failures as temporary setbacks and learning experiences rather than definitive outcomes.

I've had my fair share of failures and disappointments in my entrepreneurial journey. But I've learned to view them as stepping stones rather than stumbling blocks. I recall launching a product that could have done better than expected. Instead of getting disheartened, I sought feedback, learned from the experience, and used it to improve the product. The product eventually became one of our best sellers.

As we conclude this section, take a moment to reflect on these transformative strategies. Remember, not the strongest survive, but those most responsive to change. As Queen Nefertiti exemplifies, we can harness the power of resilience and adaptability to carve out our path to success in the entrepreneurial world.

Conclusion: Stepping into the Future with the Wisdom of the Past

As we approach the end of our shared journey through this book, I want to leave you with a sense of empowerment inspired by the strength of a woman who has transcended the bounds of time - Queen Nefertiti. Though set in the distant past, her journey holds timely lessons for us as entrepreneurs striving to shape the future.

Queen Nefertiti's story is about transformation, resilience, and the audacious will to pursue a vision. Despite her challenging circumstances and constant resistance, she chose to defy conventions, steer her own path, and rewrite history in her unique style. She embraced change, wielded her influence wisely, and used her power to create a society that reflected her vision for unity and harmony.

Her journey resonates with us as entrepreneurs. Every day, we strive to transform our visions into reality, navigating the complex labyrinth of business, balancing risk with opportunity, and constantly learning and growing from our experiences. It's not an easy path, but as Nefertiti's journey tells us, it is worthwhile.

As we chart our path, we are not alone. We stand on the shoulders of those who have come before us, women like Nefertiti and countless others who have left their indelible mark on history. We carry their legacy forward, inspired by their courage, resilience, and wisdom.

In your entrepreneurial journey, I urge you to remember the essence of Queen Nefertiti's journey. Embrace change, be willing to adapt, harness your unique strengths, and above all, dare to pursue your vision relentlessly.

As we close this chapter, let us look ahead with renewed purpose and determination. To facilitate this, here are five actionable steps that you can take moving forward:

1. **Identify Your Vision:** What is your unique vision for your enterprise? What do you want to create, change, or contribute to? Your vision will be your guiding light, so ensure it aligns with your values and passions.

2. **Embrace Change:** In the dynamic world of entrepreneurship, change is the only constant. Practice agili-

ty and keep an open mind. Remember that every change brings opportunities.

3. **Foster a Learning Culture:** As an entrepreneur, strive to be a lifelong learner. Encourage your team to do the same. Invest in skill-building and personal growth.

4. **Build Emotional Resilience:** Entrepreneurship is as much a mental game as a practical one. Develop emotional resilience to handle stress and challenges. Practice mindfulness and self-care.

5. **Make a Difference:** Entrepreneurship isn't just about profit. It's about making a difference in your own unique way. As you grow your business, consider how you can contribute positively to your community and society.

In conclusion, let the journey of Queen Nefertiti serve as a beacon of inspiration for you as you carve out your own path in the entrepreneurial world. Remember, the strength, resilience, and wisdom you need are already within you. It's just a matter of harnessing them effectively. Go forth and create your unique legacy. Your journey is just beginning, and I can't wait to see where it takes you.

As we've journeyed through this book, there's one mantra I hope you'll carry with you: "With vision and resilience, I am the architect of my destiny." This powerful affirmation encapsulates the spirit of Queen Nefertiti's journey and our own journey as entrepreneurs. Remember, you can shape your future and make a difference. Carry this mantra with you, let it echo in your mind during times of doubt and challenge, and fuel your journey to success.

Now, with the wisdom of Nefertiti and the stories, experiences, and lessons from this book in your heart, I invite you to take action. Remember, transformation is not a passive process. It is something that requires active engagement and commitment.

Firstly, reflect on your journey so far. How have you grown and changed? What challenges have you overcome? And what strengths have you discovered within yourself? Use these reflections as fuel to continue pushing forward.

Next, set clear and specific goals for your future. What does your ideal future look like? What steps will you take to get there? Write these down and create an actionable plan to achieve them.

Also, surround yourself with a community of strong, like-minded individuals. The path to success can often feel lonely, but you are not alone. Collaborate, support, and learn from one another. You'll be surprised at the power of collective growth and success.

And finally, remember to celebrate your wins, no matter how small. Every step forward is in the right direction, and each deserves recognition.

Queen Nefertiti once built an empire. Now, it's your turn. You are unstoppable, resilient, and capable of extraordinary things. Take the first step today, and continue to build the empire of your dreams.

This is your call to action. The world is waiting for your greatness. Now go forth and unleash it!

The Unstoppable Woman's Manifesto - Final Chapter Action Steps

- **Action Step 1: Reflection**
  Take some time to reflect on your journey as a woman entrepreneur. Write down the challenges you've faced, the victories you've achieved, and the growth you've experienced. What strengths have you discovered within yourself? How have these experiences shaped you as an entrepreneur?

- **Action Step 2: Future Goal Setting**
  What does your ideal future look like? Define your future goals in clear, specific terms. Write them down, and create a roadmap for how you plan to achieve

them. Break down each goal into manageable steps to make them feel less overwhelming and more attainable.

- **Action Step 3: Building Your Community**
  You don't have to journey alone. Identify individuals or groups who align with your vision and values. Connect with them, share your aspirations, learn from their experiences, and offer your support. Write down the steps you plan to take to cultivate these relationships.

- **Action Step 4: Celebrating Success**
  Create a habit of celebrating your achievements, no matter how small they may seem. Write down three recent successes and how you will celebrate them. This boosts your motivation and builds a positive mindset that embraces growth and learning.

- **Action Step 5: Embrace the Unstoppable Spirit**
  Write a personal pledge to yourself, acknowledging your resilience, strength, and unstoppable spirit. Use this pledge as a source of motivation and inspiration whenever you face challenges or feel doubtful about your journey.

- **Action Step 6: Take the First Step**
  Identify the first step you'll take in your action plan and set a date to complete it. Remember, every journey starts with a single step. Writing it down makes

it tangible and increases the likelihood of following through. Remember the story of Queen Nefertiti and her transformative journey. Let it inspire you as you make your own way towards building your empire. Stay determined, stay passionate, and most importantly, stay unstoppable.

- **Action Step 7: Embracing Adaptability**
Write down one major challenge you anticipate in your entrepreneurial journey and brainstorm possible solutions. Just like Nefertiti, remember the power of adaptability in the face of unforeseen circumstances.

- **Action Step 8: Revisit Your Mantra**
Keep your personal mantra close. Write it down on post-it notes, set it as your phone wallpaper, or keep it anywhere you can see it daily. This is your personal reminder of your resilience and strength, a motivational phrase that speaks to your spirit.

- **Action Step 9: Share Your Story**
Consider sharing your story, experiences, and lessons learned with others. Just as you found inspiration in Nefertiti's story, your journey may become a beacon of inspiration for others.

- **Action Step 10: Seek Continuous Learning**
Commit to continuous learning. Identify one book, course, or seminar related to your business or per-

sonal growth that you will engage in within the next month.

By walking through these steps, you are not only paying homage to the past but creating a path for the future. Each step you take is a testament to your strength, resilience, and the unstoppable spirit you carry within you. Each day, each moment, you are writing your own story, which can inspire others just as you were inspired.

In the closing words of our shared journey, let me reach out to you directly, the woman, the queen in her own right, standing on the precipice of her unstoppable empire.

You've ventured with me through tales of past and present, personal revelations, and the powerful narrative of Queen Nefertiti. You've embraced the transformative spirit of entrepreneurship, poised to cast your own legacy in the world. And now, you stand on the brink of a new beginning, with the wisdom of the ages, the lessons learned, and the unyielding strength of your spirit to guide you forward.

Remember this: An empire isn't just the sum of its resources or economic power. It reflects the spirit that binds it together, the vision that fuels its growth, and the resilience that enables it to endure. Your empire, which you are forging with your passion and dedication, is a testament to your strength, stability, and indomitable spirit. It is as unique and as boundless as you.

You are the architect of your destiny, the queen of your domain, and the author of your own story. Your journey is a testament to the strength within you, the resilience that has carried you through adversity, and the determination that fuels your pursuit of success.

Take heart in the knowledge that the path before you, while challenging, is also ripe with opportunity. Embrace the journey with courage, knowing that every step you take is a step towards shaping your future.

Believe in the power of your dreams. Believe in the power of your vision. But above all, believe in yourself. Because you are more than a dreamer. You are a doer, a builder, a creator. You are an unstoppable force destined for greatness.

Your empire awaits you. It's time to rise and claim what is rightfully yours. Like Queen Nefertiti, let your story echo through the ages, inspiring and empowering future gener-ations. Remember, your journey is more than a pursuit of success-it is a celebration of the incredible woman that you are.

Let the world see you in all your glory. Let your light shine. Let your spirit soar. Let your dreams guide you forward. Be unstoppable, for you are a queen, and your empire awaits.

Go forth, command, and conquer, for the world is ready for the magnificence of your reign. Be proud. Be strong. Be unstoppable. After all, you are building an empire and commanding its growth with the strength, grace, and indomitable spirit of a queen.

And always remember, as I've said before, "She who dares to conquer dares to rule." You have dared; now is your time to rule. This is your unstoppable manifesto. Embrace, live, and let it guide you to the height of your dreams.

With all my love and unyielding belief in your power,

Rochel Marie Lawson
The Queen of Feeling Fabulous

An Abundance of Gratitude

I have been inspired to write this book for my Divine team with deep appreciation and heartfelt gratitude.

I thank the Divine and my Divine team for inspiring, empowering, and guiding me to embark upon this project. I have always had a deep connection to the history of ancient Egypt, and I have always had a connection to Queen Nefertiti. This project is not an accident because diving timing is always perfect. It is my honor to be the element that shares the light of being a Queen and commanding with women and men worldwide.

I give thanks to all my family and friends who have supported me and created the space for me to have the time to write this book and have allowed me the private time that I need to get in "the essence and light" of Queen Nefertiti to channel her wisdom so that I could include it in this book.

I am grateful to all the mentors and women leaders who helped me see what I could not see in myself and for myself. These fabulous ladies were necessary to create and implement my vision for my empire and bring it to fruition strategically and successfully. Every ounce of wisdom bestowed upon me has led me to be the successful woman I am today and a queen who continually builds, commands, and expands her empire.

My Australian Shepard, Beamer, has been my backbone of emotional support. When I would get frustrated with myself as I worked on this project, he would come up, give me kisses, and lean against me, letting me know that I could count on him for support. These precious moments allowed channels of love to open inside me and fill me with the light to get deeper with my connection to what I wanted to share as I connected with the essence of Queen Nefertiti.

The support team that I have is fantastic. These fabulous behind-the-scenes team members allow me to focus on the purpose of my businesses and work on implementing strategies to take them to an elevated level, which lets more companies and people be served. My team has allowed me to be everywhere and have my businesses run seamlessly. Such a wonderful blessing!

Thank you to the Black CEO team that introduced me to the publisher, which opened the gateway for this fantastic adventure to begin. I have nothing but love for everyone at Black CEO.

Heartfelt gratitude to my publisher Zachariah, who got me the vision and message I wanted to create and share with this book. It was like we were divinely put together. Zachariah was patient, kind, understanding, and connected to every aspect of this project towards my success. We will forever be linked.

Thank you to those who have reviewed the book, endorsed the book, and supported the launch. Your kindness means the world to me. Your support helps spread the word to get more books into the hands of queens, building, expanding, and commanding their empires.

And YOU. My reader. You have taken a bold step in building and commanding your throne. I applaud you for not only seeking wisdom to live the best life possible but also understanding that the wisdom of life and business comes from all sources, even those that are no longer on this earthly plane. You have not only given yourself a wonderful gift, but you have also given yourself a gift that keeps on giving, a resource that will guide you like the queen you are as you command your empire. By tapping into the essence of Queen Nefertiti, I have been able to share with you how one of the most powerful and successful queens of ancient Egypt commanded her throne. And now I gifted you that wisdom so you can command your throne like the queen you are and have always meant to be.

ABOUT THE AUTHOR

Rochel Marie Lawson, affectionately known as "The Queen of Feeling Fabulous," embodies resilience and ambition. She is a trailblazer who has never let the status quo define her path. Struggling to find employment as an Electrical Engineer in the male-dominated landscape of Silicon Valley in the 1980s, Lawson launched her own telecommunications company, a first by a woman. Her determination and vision led to her pioneering a new frontier, breaking barriers, and setting an example for women in tech and beyond.

Rochel Marie's journey did not stop there. With an innate desire to serve others and her natural inclination towards health and well-being, she chose to expand her expertise in health and wellness by training as a Registered Nurse. Her experience in the Emergency Department fortified her resilience and exposed her to a wide range of health crises, deepening her understanding of the importance of wellness in a stressful, fast-paced world.

A true entrepreneur at heart, she did not leave her understanding of health and wellness confined to the hospital's walls. Instead, she extended her reach to the community, leveraging her comprehensive knowledge of wellness, wisdom, and wealth to guide individuals toward balanced, successful lives. Her story is a testament to her indomitable spirit and enduring commitment to empowering others, particularly women.

Her extensive experience and expertise have not only enabled her to pen down "The Unstoppable Woman's Manifesto" but also to serve as a role model for those who aspire to balance their career and personal life while maintaining their health. Rochel Marie's legacy is a beacon for any woman seeking to redefine her success, transform her dreams into reality, and foster a thriving, sustainable business. In essence, Rochel Marie Lawson is not just the Queen of Feeling Fabulous; she is a queen of overcoming challenges and turning them into opportunities.

THE BRAVE, BOLD, & UNSTOPPABLE Women's Summit™

Unleash your potential and conquer the world.
Join me for an unforgettable gathering of extraordinary speakers.
Ignite your unstoppable spirit at **THE BRAVE, BOLD, & UN-STOPPABLE Women's Summit™**

Best Selling Books

For more information on these great reads and best-selling author Rochel Marie Lawson's books, visit blissfulliving4u.com

UNLOCK THE ENERGY OF
MANIFESTING YOUR DREAMS
WITH THE
Dream Without Limitation
Journal
FOR FREE
WHEN YOU VISIT
www.blissfulliving4u.com